Advance praise for *Faith under Fire*

"Superb. In a world that can seem increasingly hopeless, *Faith under Fire* is a bright beacon of hope. In this brief but absorbing book, Matt Archbold has compiled stories that will leave any reader uplifted, inspired, consoled, and enriched. These are stories of our time that will remain timeless—and I know I'll be turning to them again and again for my preaching as great examples of faith and hope. Thank you, Matt, for reminding us that faith under fire can be forged into something beautiful."
—DEACON GREG KANDRA, award-winning journalist and multimedia editor of the *Catholic Near East Welfare Association*

"Despair is one of the devil's greatest weapons. If Satan can't make us abandon belief in God logically, he can worm his way into our psyches by showing us as much darkness as possible. Matt Archbold has put together a refreshing set of stories that remind us of the words of John's Gospel: "The light shines in the darkness, and the darkness has not overcome it.""
—MATT SWAIM, communications director of the Coming Home Network and author, *Prayer in the Digital Age* and *Your College Faith: Own It!*

"In an age of people running for safe spaces, trembling at the news, and jumping at their own shadows, Matt Archbold has given us a wonderful gift with this splendid collection of stories of Christian courage. They remind us that in every age, people have been afraid, but in every age, God has poured out the boldness of Christ into the hearts of his saints by the power of the Holy Spirit too. Read this book and be encouraged to follow Christ with moxie."
—MARK P. SHEA, author, *By What Authority?: An Evangelical Discovers Catholic Tradition*

"Matt Archbold's book *Faith under Fire* highlights the urgent need for a national conversation about—and defense of—religious liberty, the bedrock of our nation. Archbold powerfully explains the ongoing instances where Christians are facing persecution for living out their religious convictions—an all-too-common reality in recent years. For me, the most powerful stories in this book recognize the sacredness and dignity of every human life, both inside the womb and out."
—MARJORIE DANNENFELSER, president of the Susan B. Anthony List

"You won't hear about the heroes profiled in this book on the evening news. Those held up as 'heroes' or examples of 'courage' in today's world are often at odds with our Christian faith. But it takes real courage to stand strong in the face of injustice, violence, and the unknown. In this inspiring book, Matt Archbold tells the moving stories of Christians who held onto their faith, even under the most trying of circumstances. A gifted reporter and storyteller, Archbold makes these true stories come to life. Check it out—*Faith under Fire* will light a fire in your faith!"
—DANIELLE BEAN, author, editor of *Catholic Digest* magazine

"In a world of growing religious apathy and anti-religious antipathy, both secular and governmental, these stirring stories of faith and love in action, even at the risk of life and liberty, may inspire a generation that may be asked for even more."
—PATRICK ARCHBOLD, co-creator of the *Creative Minority Report*

"*Faith under Fire* includes powerful stories about Jill Stanek, Dr. George Isajiw, Catherine Adair, and Jessica Chominski. Each of these individuals made great personal sacrifices to defend unborn children. These stories will doubtless inspire not only Christians, but people of all faith traditions to defend the sanctity of all human life."
—MICHAEL NEW, visiting associate professor, department of economics, Ave Maria University

FAITH UNDER FIRE
Dramatic Stories of Christian Courage

MATTHEW ARCHBOLD

servant
AN IMPRINT OF
FRANCISCAN MEDIA
Cincinnati, Ohio

Cover design by Candle Light Studio
Book design by Mark Sullivan

LIBRARY OF CONGRESS CATALOGING-IN-PUBLICATION DATA
Names: Archbold, Matthew, author.
Title: Faith under fire : dramatic stories of Christian courage / Matthew Archbold.
Description: Cincinnati : Servant, 2016. | Includes bibliographical references.
Identifiers: LCCN 2016013255 | ISBN 9781632530943 (pbk.)
Subjects: LCSH: Courage—Religious aspects—Christianity. | Christian biography.
Classification: LCC BV4647.C75 A73 2016 | DDC 270.8/30922—dc23
LC record available at http://lccn.loc.gov/2016013255

ISBN 978-1-63253-094-3

Published by Servant
an imprint of Franciscan Media
28 W. Liberty St.
Cincinnati, OH 45202
www.FranciscanMedia.org

Printed in the United States of America.
Printed on acid-free paper.
16 17 18 19 20   5 4 3 2 1

*This book is dedicated to
my wonderful wife, Christie,
and my children
MC, Tin, Shan, Con, and Bridge.*

CONTENTS

INTRODUCTION

The way of the cross is unavoidably uphill.

Christians don't get to carry their cross downhill. Suffering has always been inextricably linked with Christianity, but those who carry their cross willingly in these times can serve as an example and inspiration to all of us.

These are not stories of saints in sandals or martyrs in the lion's den of old. These are modern stories of practicing Christians who—faced with the prospect of pain, persecution, or even death—chose faith and love. These people are not perfect. But God does not only call upon great saints to reveal his love for the world. He also calls the broken and desperate. We are all called to act as God's light in this darkening world. These are stories of those who, for at least one moment, reflected the brilliant light of God's love in a world sometimes unwilling to see it.

The story of the spread of Christianity is improbable, to say the least. How twelve men changed the world by preaching the most improbable message of all absolutely defies the imagination. It is incredible how this simple message of love transformed the world and continues to change people's lives every day, proving that Christ's redemption of us not only occurred a millennia ago but still occurs every day in hearts and souls in every part of the world. And his strengthening of our flagging faith in the face of persecution occurs even now.

The stories in this book reveal a world that can seem increasingly dark, and I fear that things will grow darker still in the years to come. And yet these stories also reveal what happens when darkness encounters light: The light is not extinguished at all. It just appears brighter in the advancing darkness.

History is replete with the horrors of Christian persecution. But those willing to stand for the faith serve as an inspiration to others to grow in their faith. Becoming a Christian is never a safe choice. Our time is no exception. Christians have become a punch line in the rhetoric of secular media. Both here and to an even greater extent on a global scale, Christians have become targets of cynical politicians, secularist lawyers, and radical terrorist groups marching under the banner of death. Many seek to intimidate Christians in order to eliminate their influence, vilifying and marginalizing their beliefs and practices, while others around the globe seek to eradicate Christians altogether. Yet miraculously, people still stand up for their faith and act out of love when few expect it.

Because nothing so confuses the world as much as an act of love, their stories often go misunderstood or untold. But I believe these miracles of faith happen more often than we think...but not always in the way we anticipate. God's miracles don't necessarily change the world so much as reveal it. And our response to them reveals who we are.

I am writing this while sitting in the living room of our house in Jeffersonville, Pennsylvania, watching a swirl of hawks soar above my five children, who are playing basketball, army, and jump rope on the lawn and the driveway. They've been sent outside by their mother and likely feel banished: They were joking as much when they filed out. Mom said that Dad needs to finish his book.

I am sure it would be little comfort to them to know I am writing this book for them and others like them. People have often asked me what the book is about, and I tell them it's hard to explain. I tell them that this is not a book about a gunman who attacked a schoolhouse; it's about the little girl who sacrificed herself for her classmates. This book isn't about abortion, but about the doctor who dedicated his life to helping women with crisis pregnancies. And this isn't about the radical terrorists who kill, but about those who choose love over life.

This is a book about hope and faith and light, and while it includes some terrible events, in the end it is, I believe, a hopeful book about love in a world that's often surprised and sometimes even opposed to those who show it. These stories remind us that we are a broken and scattered people and that only by reflecting God's light can we find our way back to each other and the one who created us and loves us. That is why I think it is so important to share them.

So when I'm asked what this book is about, I'll say it's about love because love changes lives, and only love can save the world. And these are stories of love.

CHAPTER ONE

Angels atop Schoolhouses
The West Nickel Mines Amish School

No one has greater love than this, to lay down one's life
for one's friends.

—John 15:13

In April of 2007, just days after a mass shooting had torn apart the lives of so many at Virginia Tech, a small group of Amish people from Nickle Mines, Pennsylvania, arrived carrying a wooden box containing a handmade comfort quilt to offer consolation to families, along with a framed history of the quilt and a painted picture of the West Nickle Mines schoolhouse. A letter accompanied the quilt, expressing that they had "felt the same emotions of disbelief, a sense of helplessness, anger, despair, and depression."

The quilt itself contained phrases, such as "We are blessed" and "We are thankful," to offer hope, understanding, and a reminder of God's love.

Few could understand the pain of the families in the Virginia Tech community better than those who delivered the quilt. As they handed it to the administrators of the college, it was impossible not to think back to that day just months earlier when we first heard of Nickle Mines.

I can still remember hearing about the school shooting in Amish country in Pennsylvania in 2006. It happened not too far from my own home. I hugged my children a little tighter that night. I think many of us did. The country was shocked, but in the end, I think that what most of us remember about that dreadful incident is the amazing forgiveness from the families of the victims.

This isn't a story about a terribly violent act but about an unbelievable act of sacrifice and an inspiring act of forgiveness. This isn't a story that ends with a tragedy but with miracles. This is a story than ends with love and reaching out to others. This is a beautiful story that I wish never happened.

• • •

On a crisp clear autumn morning in October 2006, Charles Carl Roberts IV, a lean six-foot-two, thirty-two-year-old milk truck driver with buzzed brown hair, drove home from his early morning shift. He arrived early enough to walk his two children to the bus stop along with his wife. As his children climbed on the bus, he suddenly and desperately called them back off the bus. He knelt down, grabbed them, and held them tightly for a few moments. He whispered urgently to each of them, "Remember, Daddy loves you."

Roberts returned home to an empty house and wrote confused and rambling suicide notes to his wife, who went to a meeting at their church. The notes detailed how he'd molested younger relatives many years before. He admitted to having urges to molest young girls now. He talked about losing faith and how he was angry at God for how his baby, Elise, died nine years before, just twenty minutes after being born prematurely. He apologized to his children for not being there to watch them grow up.

Roberts then climbed into the pickup truck he'd borrowed from his wife's father and drove, occasionally passing the small horse-drawn buggies of the Amish who make their home on the green rolling hills dotted with Holstein cattle and weathered barns. He didn't drive far on those thin country roads before passing the white pasture fence and then up about 150 feet to a small, cream-colored building.

It was the West Nickle Mines Amish School.

In the truck, Roberts had a 9 mm pistol (purchased three years before in a local gun shop), a shotgun, a rifle, a stun gun, two knives, smokeless powder, six hundred rounds of ammunition, and a five-gallon bucket filled with tools that included a hammer, a hacksaw, pliers, rolls of clear tape, eyebolts, lubricants, a hose, bullets, guns, binoculars, earplugs, flashlights, wood, candles, and a change of clothes. He'd planned well for an extended hell on earth for the little school.

Roberts walked into the schoolhouse unannounced during the German and spelling lessons wearing a baseball cap and holding a piece of metal in his hand. He asked the teacher, twenty-year-old Emma Mae Zook, if she'd seen another one like it nearby.

It was his mannerisms that disturbed Emma Mae. He stood too close to her. He spoke quietly and wouldn't meet her eyes, instead looking down. She promised the strange man that she and the children would look out for it, and she felt relieved as he walked outside to his pickup truck.

But moments later, he came back with a shotgun. Emma Mae quickly made eye contact with her mother, who was visiting the school that day, and they immediately both ran out the nearby side door. Roberts saw his plan unraveling fast. He ordered a boy out the door, telling him to chase down the women and bring them back, or he would start shooting. The boy ran out, but Emma Mae didn't stop running until she reached a nearby farmhouse to call the authorities. The boy didn't return either.

Roberts, in a panic, then quickly began pulling down all the shades over the windows, getting ready for an assault he knew would be coming soon. As one of the shades snapped back up, he fumbled with it. That was when Emma Fisher heard a voice.

An urgent whisper. "Now would be a good time to run," said the voice.

And so, she did. She fled to the door, and she didn't stop. She still doesn't know who whispered those words to her. To this day Emma wonders why she heard the voice telling her to leave. She wonders why she survived. Her mother told reporters that she and the boys who left the schoolhouse struggle with that even now.

Some have suggested that it might have been an angel who whispered those words to her. But whoever it was, her decision to run that day probably saved her life. Her two older sisters, Marian, thirteen, and Barbie, eleven, were still in the room. They had another, more important job to do.

Roberts may have known the Fisher girls because he picked up milk at their family farm. Marian Fisher worked hard on the farm. She worked hard on her studies. She loved Jesus the way her family had taught her. She didn't watch television, so she probably didn't know that there were two school shootings earlier that week in other parts of the country.

Roberts now focused his plans. Looking at the group in the schoolhouse, Roberts announced to the older women, "You ladies can leave; those with the children." His focus was squarely on the young girls.

He was talking to Emma Mae's sister-in-law, Sarah, twenty-three, who had remained behind in the classroom. She had her two-year-old daughter and newborn son with her. Her sister, Lydia Mae, twenty-one, who was eight months pregnant, and her sixteen-year-old sister, Ruth Ann, had also stayed.

They all stood to leave. She looked out at the ten girls huddled together in the classroom. She can still recall one of the girls, seven-year-old Naomi Rose, looking up at her with fear in her eyes. In response, Lydia Mae could only put her hands together in prayer.

Naomi Rose had cried to stay home from school that morning,

but her brothers had talked her into going.

Lydia Mae stood there staring at the little girl until Roberts screamed at her again to leave. She wasn't sure what to do, but despite the evil intentions this man had brought with him, she said she sensed the presence of God in that little classroom.

The women walked outside. They couldn't bring themselves to go far, though, and waited in the playground. They said they looked back at the school and saw an angel hovering above the schoolhouse.

As they stood there, the door opened once again. Roberts sent all the boys out. They ran out and gathered in a nearby meadow. They were all asking each other questions and figuring out what to do when they heard it. At first they didn't understand what they were hearing. They heard pounding—savage and hurried pounding. With everyone but the little girls gone, Roberts was nailing barricades across the doors and windows. He was now alone with the ten girls.

Roberts arranged the girls, including Marian Fisher, her sister, and three teacher's aides, in front of the blackboard and tied them up tightly together.

Because a call had been placed to police from a nearby farm by escaped teacher Emma Mae Zook just nine minutes before, State troopers arrived at the schoolhouse at 10:45 AM and set up a perimeter. The police quickly spoke to the adults and children who had escaped and gathered outside. The police learned quickly what they were up against, and they strategized and talked about communication options while some of the troopers readied ballistic shields, as they feared that rushing the building was the only way this was going to end.

Just before 11:00 AM, Roberts's wife returned home. She'd come home from a prayer meeting and discovered his rambling suicide note. She tried desperately and repeatedly to reach him on his cell phone. Nothing. When she'd finally given up, her phone rang. It was her husband. He told her calmly, "I am not coming home. The police are here."

Roberts hung up and then called 911. The static on the line made it difficult for them to hear Roberts. "Hello," the dispatcher said. "Lancaster County 911, do you need police, fire, or ambulance? Hello. Your cell phone is cutting in and out. Do you have an emergency?"

Roberts said he did. When the dispatcher asked him the address, he began to answer and then stopped.

According to the *Philadelphia Inquirer*, he said, "I just took, uh, ten girls hostage and I want everybody off the property or...or else."

"OK, all right," the dispatcher said, trying to calm Roberts down.

"Now!" screamed Roberts.

"OK, what's the problem there?" asked the dispatcher.

Roberts interrupted again, screaming, "Don't try to talk me out of it, get them all off the property now!"

The dispatcher asked Roberts to hold while transferring the call to the state police on the scene. "Sir, I want you to stay on the phone with me, OK? I'm going to let the State Police down there...I need to let you talk to them. OK, can I transfer you to them?"

Roberts refused. "No, you tell them and that's it. Right now or they're dead, in two seconds. Two seconds—that's it!" he screamed.

The dispatcher attempted to speak, saying, "Sir, listen to me. Listen..." But Roberts hung up. The police negotiator just outside the school desperately redialed Roberts but was unable to get through. Roberts, feeling that the police were sure to dash toward the school at any moment, readied himself to commit an unspeakable act of horror. He would begin shooting the girls.

That was when it happened—a miracle. Not the kind that

changed anything in that schoolhouse, but one that affected the millions of us outside the schoolhouse. Thirteen-year-old Marian Fisher raised her voice. "Shoot me first and leave the other ones loose," she said.

Her eleven-year-old sister, Barbie, then said, "Shoot me next."

"Shoot me first." Imagine saying those words. Now listen to them again in your mind. Then imagine them being said by a child.

Marian Fisher and her sister Barbie must have known the police were coming from Roberts's frantic phone calls, and they may have believed that if they offered themselves, perhaps he wouldn't have time to kill the others. This was a moment that we should all measure ourselves against.

Roberts looked strangely at the girls, and he asked them to pray for him just before he opened fire. The police heard the shots and raced toward the school. First, he killed Marian Fisher instantly and severely wounded her sister Barbie. She received bullet wounds in the leg, hand, and shoulder. Five girls died; five others were critically injured.

Police heard the quick shots ring out as ten troopers stormed the school. But police couldn't break through the barricades fashioned from used lumber, flexible plastic ties, and furniture. Police used everything they had to gain entrance into the school. They used their shields, the butts of rifles, and batons to punch their way in through windows and doors even as Roberts began shooting at the officers.

The troopers bravely charged in with little regard for their own safety and ended up saving five of the ten girls. As the first of the troopers gained entrance, Roberts turned the gun on himself.

• • •

Finally, there was silence. A terrible silence. The police were horrified at what they encountered. The county's deputy coroner, Janice Ballenger, reportedly said, "There was not one desk, not one chair, in the whole schoolroom that was not splattered with either blood or glass. There were bullet holes everywhere…everywhere."

Police almost immediately discovered two students and a teacher's aide mortally wounded. Little Naomi Rose, who hadn't wanted to go to school that day, died in a policeman's arms just outside the school.

Marian Fisher was dead, but five of her classmates survived the assault that day, including her sister Barbie, who told her family what happened from her bed at Children's Hospital of Philadelphia, where she was treated for wounds to her shoulder, hand, and leg.

The headlines that night screamed, "Gunmen Kills Amish Children" and "School Shooting in Pennsylvania," but something remarkable, even miraculous, happened in that one-classroom schoolhouse: an act of bravery that gave millions pause.

Marian Fisher exhibited that hope and faith can still outshine the darkness of evil. However dense the darkness may appear, our hope for the triumph of the light is stronger still. Though violence continues to stain us with blood, the shadows of death can be dissipated with one act of light.

Darkness faced light on that perfectly clear morning in Nickle Mines, Pennsylvania. Light won. It won out over heartbreak and tragedy. It won out over fear and hatred. The stories from the media began focusing on Marian's heroism. The nightly news talked about it. Her story gave America something to hold on to after such a dark event. It reminded us of something we'd always known—that evil will always exist, and it will enter our lives unexpectedly and without consent. But how deeply that darkness will touch us is up to us; our will is our own. The dark affects our bodies but not necessarily our souls. Our lives can be taken. But they can also be given. Marian and Barbie Fisher remind us of that.

• • •

"Where did they get that courage?" people might ask themselves. That's the kind of question we can't really answer. Surely, the faith handed down to her from her family was pure and strong. But there was surely something more at work here—courage, faith, and the work of the Holy Spirit. Marian Fisher bore witness to her faith in Christ by sacrificing her own life to save others, just as her family bore witness by finding strength to forgive.

While the world was outraged over the tragedy, the media descended into the tiny town seeking to fill their stories the way they've done with now, sadly, dozens of others—stories of anger, desperation, a call for gun control, and a desire for revenge. But the families of the victims did what so many found inexplicable. The Fisher family invited Roberts's widow to the private funeral and were quoted in the newspaper as saying they knew how difficult it must be for Mrs. Roberts and her children, and they wanted to extend their support to them.

The family didn't speak much to the press, but Dwight Lefever, a Roberts family spokesman, said Amish neighbors comforted the Roberts family hours after the shooting and extended forgiveness to them.

Dozens of Amish neighbors attended Charles Roberts's funeral on October 7, 2006. Roberts's wife was touched by the outward gesture of forgiveness by the Amish community.

The country was stunned. "The togetherness of the Amish is very unique, and they look to each other for support," said Rita Rhoads, a Mennonite midwife who delivered two of the shooting victims. "They really want the world to know that they have forgiven the shooter," Rhoads said as she stood along the road Thursday waiting for the funeral buggies to pass. "They definitely are very upset for him and his family. They view him as a community member just like the children."

Soon, many of the stories on the news and in newspapers focused on Marian Fisher's sacrifice and the forgiveness shown by the families. Thousands of people were so moved by the goodness surrounding this heartbreaking incident that donations came pouring in from around the country, adding up to over three million dollars to be used for medical expenses, long-term care, counseling, and transportation. The group in charge of donations added it had been in contact with Roberts's widow, Marie, "to make sure adequate support was available" for her and their three children.

On the night of the funeral, the families of Marian Fisher and other victims that night invited the Roberts family to join them in grief and remembrance. They opened the doors of their hearts to the family of their children's murderer. How many families could think that way just hours after losing children?

The Fisher family is an example of the words of St. Paul: "Do not be overcome by evil, but overcome evil with good" (Romans 12:21).

Evil came to a one-room schoolhouse in Pennsylvania that day. Yet goodness prevailed. Days later, Lydia Mae, the pregnant woman who was told to leave the school, delivered a six-pound, four-ounce baby girl. She named her Naomi Rose.

When violence and suffering threaten to overwhelm us, we must pray for the grace to be such beacons of hope and goodness in a fallen world. By working to restore hope through the daily choice to forgive and live in love, as the Fisher family did, we take a bold stand against the culture of death.

The night after her older sister Marian was buried, little Emma Fisher had a dream. Marian appeared to her in heaven. So did her uncle, who had died of cancer; his firstborn, Reuben, a crib-death victim; and her great-grandfather. She had never laid eyes on the latter three, but she insisted she recognized them all. They came to say that everything was all right. They were with God.

In April 2007, many members of the Amish community reached out to the families of the victims of the Virginia Tech shooting by traveling to Blacksburg, Virginia, to pass along a comfort quilt.

We are a country of contradictions. We are a nation, which, sadly, is no longer, surprised by the murder of innocents but are shocked at the bravery of a thirteen-year-old girl and the forgiveness of her family and community. Horror surrounds us. Forgiveness astounds us.

We understand that what Marian Fisher and the entire Fisher family did was miraculous, and we stand in awe. Maybe our salvation lies in that. We still recognize the light. We still recognize angels sitting atop schoolhouses and even the little ones inside.

DISCUSSION QUESTIONS

1. Can you think of an example in your own life where someone you know acted unselfishly in order to protect others?

2. What does the reaction of this Amish community teach us about how to begin the process of reconciliation when someone wrongs us?

3. When you encounter evil, how do you most often respond? In this story, several of those in the schoolhouse chose to stay with the younger ones, putting themselves in danger. Was this the only "right" option?

CHAPTER TWO

The Triumph over Emptiness

Sr. Laura Mainetti

Let all bitterness and wrath and anger and clamor and
slander be put away from you, along with all malice. Be
kind to one another, tenderhearted, forgiving one another,
as God in Christ forgave you.

—Ephesians 4:31–32

It all began in the spring of 2000 in the idyllic town of Chiavenna,
Italy, a prosperous town of seven thousand inhabitants near
Lake Como, on the border between Italy and Switzerland.
Bored with small-town life, three teenage girls named Ambra,
Veronica, and Milena entered into a satanic pact, seeking to drum
up a little excitement. As heavy metal music screamed and pulsed,
the girls cut their hands and wrists, poured their blood into a glass,
and drank it to strengthen their allegiance and bind themselves
irreversibly to their secret cause. Then, under the cover of darkness, the girls broke into a local church, stole a Bible, and burnt it.

A few months later, on June 6, the undercurrent of evil erupted
into unspeakable horror. Late that night the same three girls placed
a call to the local convent of the Congregation of the Daughters of
the Cross. It was the sixth day of the sixth month; the significance
of this eluded police for weeks. Sr. Laura answered the phone,
and one of the girls claimed a friend had been raped, was now

12

pregnant, and needed help. She insisted that Sr. Laura meet the girl at a nearby secluded park. Sr. Laura, sixty, rushed out of the convent at 10:30 PM to offer help. Sr. Laura never returned.

• • •

It was likely the sister didn't suspect any danger. In any case, it was unlikely that she would have turned a deaf ear. By telling the nun of a pregnancy, the girls had appealed to a soft spot in the heart of Sr. Laura, whose own mother died shortly after giving birth to her.

Sr. Laura had dedicated her life to helping those in need and on the margins of society: drug addicts and prostitutes, the forgotten ones and the young. After thirty years of service, Sr. Laura was well known for her social and charitable commitment to the young, dispossessed, and poor. She considered the youth the real poor of today, and she often commented that the youngest generation were lost and given very little direction by adults. She feared for their spiritual safety.

As Sr. Laura arrived in the park, Veronica beckoned her into a secluded and dark pathway, where Ambra and Milena lay concealed in shadow. Sr. Laura walked bravely into the darkness. A few minutes later, three girls hurriedly abandoned the area. Amber threw a stone in a nearby stream, where Milena cleaned blood from her shoes and Veronica busily washed the bloody knife in a nearby fountain. The girls were seen later that night at an amusement park, acting like the sixteen- and seventeen-year-old girls they were—as if nothing at all had happened.

The following morning a passerby discovered the body. Sr. Laura had been stabbed nineteen times.

News of the horrible crime spread quickly across the small town by word of mouth. Soon the eyes of Europe fell upon the town, which up to that time was not known for any crimes more serious than trivial vandalism or minor theft. Within twenty-four hours the largest European dailies all prominently featured the mysterious murder of the nun. One channel ran a news special on the murder. At first, the police sought out the drug addicts and prostitutes who had most recently received help from the sisters. But a witness testified to police that she'd seen the nun on the night of the murder walking with a young girl and described her. Soon after, DNA tests from hair and skin found under the fingernails of Sr. Laura traced the murder to a troubled young girl who lived in the town. The police soon tapped the cell phones of the three friends and overheard damning conversations, including one saying, "I have had my hair cut so the police will never recognize me."

"They will never catch us because they don't know who we are," reassured another.

One of the things that shocked police was that the girls, despite a few conversations concerning the police investigation, carried on as if nothing had happened. The girls sat for their exams, hung out in the piazza, and went clubbing on weekends. When the police finally knocked on their door twenty-one days after the murder, the girls' parents were stunned.

For four hours of relentless questioning, the girls all calmly denied involvement until police showed them the transcripts of their recorded phone conversations. Suddenly, two of the girls burst into tears, while another reportedly responded simply that it had all been a game.

Newspapers and television shows discussed "the game" the girls were playing and attempted to put the crime into some form of societal context. But the chief of the local public prosecutor's office, Gianfranco Avella, said that while the girls had been charged with the nun's murder, he remained unconvinced by their stated motive. He didn't believe it was a game.

After continuing his investigation, Avella discovered occult scribblings in the girls' schoolbooks and journals. He found death metal

CDs like those of Marilyn Manson, an avowed Satanist. Police put that information together with the date of the murder being the sixth day of the sixth month, one short of 666, the numeric symbol for the devil.

Confronted with this information, the girls from their prison cells began elaborating about their dark motives and about how far Satanism's grip had reached into the small town.

Investigators revealed that in their numerous searches carried out in the homes of several middle class families, they discovered the existence of a surprisingly strong satanic subculture present in the children of good, stable, and well-respected families. Many other girls had taken place in Bible burnings, blood oaths, and other rituals. From prison, Milena confirmed Avella's worst fears. To his questions, she answered bluntly, "Satan had ordered us to kill."

Vatican journalist Sandro Magister said in an interview shortly after the murder, "Satan is back. But in his way, he´s always been there. June 6, 2000, was another of his darkest and most devious days in Italy." He said many of today's youth are "lured by fashionable forms of Satanism."

Investigators later learned that the three girls initially wanted to sacrifice a priest in their satanic rite—and their first choice was the pastor of the local church, Monsignor Ambrogio Balatti, but they feared that he might be too strong, so they sought to carry out their satanic blood ritual against Sr. Laura.

Satanism and occultism had been a growing fad in Italy and throughout Europe, according to Monsignor Balatti. "Dress, music and some books contributed to the spread of such a tendency.... It found fertile ground in some because they were angry with God, perhaps because of personal problems, because of family troubles."

After much questioning and investigation, the girls themselves told what they did to Sr. Laura the night they made their macabre sacrifice to Satan.

The three murderers lured the kindly nun into the alleyway when one of the girls jumped out, striking the nun in the back of the head with a stone to force her to the ground. The girls forced the nun to kneel, as a gesture of submission, in compliance with the symbolic ritual. They then made use of two knives to carry out their rite. The girls tried to stab her eighteen times (6+6+6, a symbolic number), but in the excitement, they failed to keep proper count and added an extra one. The sixty-year-old nun fought hard. But eventually her blood loss made fighting impossible.

And what did Sr. Mainetti do as she was dying? She didn't cry to be spared. She didn't scream at them or curse. She looked up to heaven, prayed for her murderers, and granted them her forgiveness. "Lord, forgive them," were her last words as the girls viciously delivered the fatal wounds.

Bishop Alessandro Maggiolini called the grisly murder "the triumph of emptiness." But the triumph, in the end, was God's because this saintly woman prayed for the girl's forgiveness even as she felt her life being taken from her. This moment, in truth, was the triumph of faith over emptiness. This action by the victim in this murder gave the moment its meaning.

According to recent news reports, the young murderers have shown signs of being repentant, partly due to Sr. Mainetti's heroic prayer as she was dying.

On August 9, 2001, Ambra had the case against her dismissed on the grounds of diminished responsibility and was sentenced to three years' rehabilitation. Because of their age, the other two girls, Milena and Veronica, were given light sentences, despite being found guilty of first degree murder.

On November 6, 2005, the cause of beatification was opened for Sr. Maria Laura Mainetti. Then Pope Benedict XVI said that Sr. Laura, "with a total giving of self, sacrificed her life while praying for those who were attacking her."

Monsignor Ambrogio Balatti observed, "After the time of sorrow and mourning, now is the moment of joy and light."

The monsignor also spoke of a prophetic conversation he'd had with Sr. Laura shortly before her death. "Lately, Sr. Mary Laura confided in me her desire to give everything. She understood that many times we give ourselves to others, but we always keep something back for ourselves. She then said that only in martyrdom do we succeed in giving everything, even our own lives. Today I read her intuitions as a premonition. They were the Lord's call, so that she would be prepared for any eventuality."

DISCUSSION QUESTIONS

1. Do you believe in Satan? What does the Church teach about the reality of evil? (See CCC 395.)
2. For many, the thought that three teenage girls from good homes would be capable of this level of violence is disturbing. What did you take from their story?
3. What can we learn from Sr. Laura about forgiveness?

CHAPTER THREE

The Hardest to Forgive
Catherine Adair

In him we have redemption through his blood, the forgiveness of our trespasses, according to the riches of his grace that he lavished on us. With all wisdom and insight he has made known to us the mystery of his will, according to his good pleasure that he set forth in Christ, as a plan for the fullness of time, to gather up all things in him, things in heaven and things on earth.

—Ephesians 1:7–10

Sometimes the hardest person to forgive is ourselves. I think we somehow convince ourselves that Christ's suffering on the cross is sufficient for everyone but us. But true faith can help us to heal. Some say faith is blind. But it seems to me that sometimes faith opens our eyes.

The room in the back of the clinic was quiet, but Catherine's mind was screaming. A baby was in that jar. Arms. Leg. Fingers! There was a baby in a jar! She knew she had to get out of there. Fast. She couldn't look at it one moment longer.

It?

Catherine Adair had spent the previous year working at Planned Parenthood convincing women that despite what they thought, that wasn't a baby growing in their womb. It was a…an…it. And it required a "procedure," as she called it back then. She accepted payment for abortions and "counseled" young women in the bright office and worked as a medical assistant for first-trimester abortions.

But one day in 1997 everything changed. She was asked to clean up the room from a second-trimester abortion. She had never been in that room before, and even though she had "counseled" other women about the procedure, she had no idea what it really entailed. She'd walked into a similar room once before when she was nineteen when she aborted her unborn baby at eleven weeks, something she promised herself a long time before she wouldn't think about ever again. And she hadn't wanted to go back in, but she convinced herself that there was nothing wrong with what was going on.

"I walked in and looked on the side table. And there's a jar. And in this jar are clearly body parts. Two arms; two legs. I stared at it. I wasn't sure if I was making it up. I felt like I was having an out-of-body experience. I backed up out of the room. I went to the medical assistant and said, 'I can't do this.'"

"What's wrong?" asked the medical assistant.

"I...I...I can't go back in there," said Catherine.

"You wanna talk about it?" asked the other woman.

"No," replied Catherine.

She didn't want to talk about it because talking about it would almost make it more real.

"I couldn't process it. It was so brutal. It was shocking. Up to that point I hadn't understood we were talking about real human beings. Arms and legs. Even though I counseled women on abortion, I had no idea. In the first trimester maybe you can believe the lie that it's not a baby but on that particular day I couldn't believe the lie anymore."

Come on Catherine, she argued with herself. *You're a feminist! You were a Women's Studies major, for goodness sake. You marched on Washington for women's rights. You believe pro-lifers like the ones who stand outside with signs are crazy.*

For Catherine the truth of what was in that jar conflicted with everything she thought she knew. "In my world back then, you were either pro-women and pro-abortion or you were crazy," she says. "I thought, 'There's something wrong with me.' So I had nobody to talk to so I just went back to work."

• • •

Somehow she showed up to work the following day, putting what she'd seen away. Burying it. Ignoring it. Catherine excelled at that. She'd had practice. She was a burier. World class. She could ignore things and pretend they never existed. So she sat down and counseled women that what was in their womb wasn't a life. It wasn't a baby. And it wasn't a surgery so much as a "procedure." She accepted payment and watched them go into the procedure room.

After a few times, she could almost start believing it all again. When she told women, "The doctor is going to extract the contents of the uterus," she could almost not think, "The doctor will have to rip the baby apart with forceps." Almost. She almost didn't think of the blood on the floor or the arms and legs.

She showed up to work each day until she could almost believe she hadn't seen what she'd seen. But then came the nightmares and the sleepless nights. There's something about nighttime that makes the truth hit harder. Truth is always more visible at 3:00 AM.

"Terrible nightmares," is how she describes it. "I'd wake up screaming because I'd seen body parts floating around."

She says she started feeling angry working at Planned Parenthood. She couldn't even admit to herself why she was angry, but for the first time, she noticed what she called hypocrisy in the people around her who claimed to be pro-woman. She couldn't help but hear the nasty things the workers said about the women who came into the clinic. She couldn't help but notice that the doctor performing abortions avoided all eye contact with the women. "Women were treated horribly," said Catherine. "And it was the most racist place I've ever been in my life."

"When a black woman walks in, there's a perception that she can't afford the baby right away," she says. "For black women they really pushed Depo-Provera, which is a shot every three months." She says her manager told her, "Don't bother giving them the pill because they never remember to take it."

Finally, she found herself so unceasingly upset and angry that she reconsidered her life. Not her positions. Instead of confronting the conflict in her heart, she simply retreated from it. All she knew was that she couldn't work at Planned Parenthood anymore. "I decided enough of this," she says. "I decided to go to grad school."

She earned her teaching certification, taught at a local school, married her college sweetheart, had children, and stayed at home with them. But when it came to her interior life, she was still apathetic about God and passionately pro-choice.

"I never expressed these negative feelings," she says. "I didn't know any pro-life people. I didn't know who to talk to."

But Catherine's husband was Catholic, and he wanted the children baptized, and he wanted to take them to Mass. Catherine wasn't so sure. She didn't exactly fight it, but she was more than comfortable church shopping. *Religion is fine for the kids, but it's best not to get muddled in the nitty-gritty of it all,* she thought.

She'd been baptized a Catholic, but her family hadn't practiced the faith much. What she knew of the Catholic Church, she wasn't crazy about. "I was very resistant to the idea of going back to the Catholic Church," she says. "I was willing to be anything but Catholic."

But when they met a charismatic priest, Fr. Emerito Ortiz, they decided to attend St. Francis of Assisi Parish. But it wasn't really being Catholic, Catherine convinced herself. She told herself she just liked the priest and attended there. For the children, she told herself.

Soon she noticed she liked the statues. And the incense. She followed along with the Mass and began to see its beauty. "I think I started there feeling like I wasn't sure if my heart was in it—you know, still thinking about the church in terms of how the secular world defines it," she says. "But I really loved the Mass, and I love the tradition—the more statues and incense the happier I am."

But still she knew that underneath the smells and bells there was that "obsession" with abortion and contraception, and she wanted no part of that.

When she heard that a CCD teacher left in the middle of the year, she volunteered to fill in. After all, she'd been a teacher. In order to teach the children, she began studying the faith. And that's where she says everything changed.

She learned about the devotions, the saints, and the teachings of the Church. And she found the Mass more meaningful in light of all she read. For the first time she could recall, she came away with the sense that she had not just engaged in a weekly ritual, but had truly encountered Christ. "Jesus really let me feel his presence in the Mass, and I knew that I was where he wanted me to be," she says.

And then surprising herself, she felt this indescribable need to go to confession. "I wanted what other people had," she says. "I really wanted to go to confession. I wanted all this off my heart."

But she was terrified. She convinced herself that nobody else in the entire world had ever done what she'd done. She told herself that no priest could ever be ready to hear such a terrible confession. Time and again she entered the church intending to go to confession—and lost the nerve to actually speak to the priest.

It was Lent in 2009 when she finally entered the confessional, and for the first time in years, she spoke of things she hadn't allowed herself to think about for so long. She told Fr. Ortiz about aborting her own child at nineteen.

"When I found out I was pregnant, I was happy. It seemed like such a miracle. A baby. Neither one of us was in a place to have a baby. We hadn't finished college. He was working as a roofer making six bucks an hour. But I thought we could make it work.

"I told my mother, and she immediately said, 'OK, abortion is legal now. You have a choice.' All of a sudden I was like, 'I can't have this baby. We can't support it. My parents won't help us.'"

She says looking back, she thinks her mother thought she was doing the right thing. "She was a feminist and thought she was helping me," she says. Her mother took her to a local doctor who made an appointment at a local clinic for her.

Instead of the miracle she first thought the baby was, she began seeing it as an eleven-week-old problem, something that the grown-ups like her doctor and her mother would handle. "I was feeling like a child," she says. "The appointment was made, I was there, and suddenly I was in the room."

She says she never felt like she had a choice.

Catherine, under general anesthesia, didn't remember the procedure. But she remembered coming out of the "procedure" room and bursting into tears. "I felt so alone," she says. "So empty."

She told Fr. Ortiz that by the time she got back to the car, she told herself that it was over. She told herself that she wasn't going to think about it again. Ever again.

That is, until she told Fr. Ortiz. "At first he didn't get what I was saying," she says. "And then he said, 'Oh.'" And then silence. Catherine braced for the scolding she knew was coming. "But he was so kind," she says. "So nonjudgmental."

At Fr. Ortiz's request, she walked out of the confessional and knelt down in a pew and prayed the fifth luminous mystery of the Eucharist. She prayed the rosary every day and soon found herself longing for the Eucharist. And she hasn't stopped saying the rosary since.

"I received on Easter. I still have chills when I think about it," she says. "It opened my heart. All these years I was so afraid, but what a gift. The Church gives us so many gifts. I felt like I was born again. He has continued to grace me and bless me in so many ways."

One day during Mass, it all hit her out of the blue. She remembered what she'd seen in that surgical room. All that she had buried came out. She remembered it all and contrasted it with the Church's beautiful stance of the sacredness of life, all life. "I started to slowly understand the Church's teaching on abortion. I always thought before it was a bit of an obsession," she says. "It was so gentle, so beautiful. God lifted the veil. It's a baby. They're babies."

She cried throughout the entire Mass and after. "I was crying for all the babies," she says. "I'd started to intellectually get it. But he put it in my heart. These babies are being killed. God had taught me little by little. He brought me in so gently."

It was shortly after that when Catherine began speaking about her own experiences. "It was the first time I could speak about it without having a breakdown," she says. Since then, she's spoken out about her abortion and her work at Planned Parenthood. Catherine says her conversion has been tough for some people in her life to accept.

"I've gotten one of two reactions. One from Christians—pure and total support, and love, and just so caring. In my personal life it's been mixed. I understand this is challenging for people. Some of my very good friends cut me out of their lives. One friend basically said, 'I can't have you in my life anymore.'"

"My biggest challenge is my family. My parents and sisters are all liberal pro-choice people who are really struggling with this," she says. "My mom didn't know my abortion had caused me difficulty. I believe at some point we'll have a conversation. I think the fact that I'm a practicing Catholic is even worse than me being pro-life."

. . .

Last year Catherine and Fr. Ortiz started the Respect Life Ministry in Fitchburg, Massachusetts, where she speaks about the value of each human life at every age. She's spoken as part of Cornerstone Action of New Hampshire and the Susan B. Anthony (SBA) List.

Few testimonies are as effective at exposing the abortion industry as those of former abortion industry employees, says SBA List President Marjorie Dannenfelser. "Coming forward this year, Catherine's brave testimony has been and will continue to be pivotal in the fight to expose and defund Planned Parenthood. The poise with which she explains her pro-life conversion, her compassion for unborn children and their mothers is all part of her incredible witness to love and mercy. Catherine has become one of our key allies in overcoming the myth that Planned Parenthood is a friend to women, and we look forward to continuing to work with her."

This past year, Catherine has been at the forefront of the pro-life movement. As part of her speaking out, Catherine wrote in the *Washington Examiner*:

> Planned Parenthood's mission is to pressure as many women into having an abortion as it can. Those in charge know that can't be accomplished if they refer to the child as a "baby."
>
> Then women would know what was really growing inside them: a little person with a beating heart, functioning nervous system, tiny hands and feet. The child is entirely disregarded. There is no counseling, no care, no waiting and no discussion. Once a pregnancy is confirmed, it is off to termination. Planned Parenthood takes specific advantage of women who are too young or misinformed to know better

than to trust them with their well-being. Those who know the truth have a duty to speak out.

After a conversion a decade in the making, that's what Catherine is intent on doing. She knows you can never really make up for lost time or lost lives, but she knows you have to try.

DISCUSSION QUESTIONS

1. Have you ever felt that there was something you'd done for which you could never forgive yourself or be forgiven?
2. Have you had any difficulties with family members over your Christianity?
3. The rosary can be a powerful tool in the battle against evil. Can you think of a time when this Catholic devotion made a difference in your life?

CHAPTER FOUR

Love That Liberates
Mother Antonia Brenner

I was naked and you clothed me, I was sick and you visited me, I was in prison and you came to me.... Truly I tell you, just as you did it to one of the least of these who are members of my family, you did it to me.

—Matthew 25:36, 40

God calls us all to holiness. No matter where we are in life, no matter what we've done, God is showing us the way even if it twists and turns in seeming darkness. Christ will never abandon us. He calls out to us, and we must respond.

The La Mesa Penitentiary in Tijuana, Mexico, was in the grip of a terrible and violent riot on Halloween night in 1994. Smoke filled the air, gunshots exploded, and bodies fell. Several fires grew unchecked in different parts of the prison.

Several inmates, protesting their treatment following the death of a prisoner, jumped some guards, ripped their guns from them, and took them as hostages. The prison, which is sometimes referred to as El Pueblito (the little town), was overcrowded with over eight thousand prisoners in a facility made for half that number, many of whom were murderers, rapists, and drug smugglers.

Amid the smoke and the screams that night, a tiny figure in white entered the prison despite the warden's warnings for her to stay outside. A tiny, frail figure walked slowly into one of the most dangerous prisons in the world set in the one of the world's most dangerous cities. She felt along the walls in the darkness, repeating all the while, *"Mis hijos"* (My Sons.)

"La Mama," came the eventual reply from a group of prisoners in the dark. They immediately assembled around her, pleading with her to leave before she got hurt. But Mother Antonia steadfastly continued into the heart of the prison even as gunshots sounded nearby.

A group of prisoners followed her, surrounding her in an effort to protect her. The group around her grew as she continued calling out *"Mis hijos."*

As she entered into the heart of the riot, many of the prisoners were shocked to see her there. She begged them to put down their guns. They gathered around her and told her that as soon as they heard her voice they tossed their guns from the windows. In a shocking display of trust, the prisoners lay down their weapons for Mother Antonia. The riot was ended. Later, she spoke to the warden on behalf of the prisoners. They knew that she would always stand with them.

Mother Antonia had lived in a ten-by-ten-foot cell in the prison for years. She ate the same food and stood for roll call with the prisoners each morning. And she was not silent on their behalf. But her ministry in the prison wasn't only to the prisoners but to the guards as well. A typical violent practice at La Mesa was for the guards to force a new prisoner to walk through a gauntlet of prison guards. The prisoner was ordered to loudly announce their name, their crime, and any aliases. If the guards didn't think they were speaking loud enough or simply didn't like what they said, the guards beat the prisoner as they walked through. To stop this, Mother Antonia began walking in each of the new prisoners, and the guards immediately ceased that practice.

• • •

As surprising as these stories are, they're hardly the most surprising thing to happen to her. Mary Clarke was born on December 1, 1926, in Los Angeles and grew up in Beverly Hills, California. Her mother died when she was very young. Her father, Joseph, was a successful salesman, and Mary grew up in the same neighborhood as Cary Grant and Heddy Lamar and rarely wanted for anything.

Life was good, but she wasn't raised to be selfish. The Catholic family often volunteered to help the poor, including sending medical supplies to impoverished countries or providing help right at home to the United Farm Workers movement.

A beauty, she caught the attention of boys from an early age and was married at eighteen. Unfortunately, her marriage didn't last long, but she had two children. A second marriage to a man named Carl Brenner, lasted about twenty-five years, but it, too, ended in divorce, but not before giving her five more children.

While raising her children, she was involved in numerous charities and ran her deceased father's business on her own. When most of her children were grown, she began expanding her charitable activities.

After a local priest invited her to travel down to Tijuana, Mexico, she was horrified by their circumstances. After visiting a number of hospitals, they visited La Mesa prison. She was shocked at the deplorable conditions. She yearned to help the inmates. Even after leaving to go back home, she wondered about them often and prayed for them.

She would return often to work in the prison, so often that the warden offered her a bed to stay overnight in. She believed she was being called.

Her youngest, still a teenager, went to live with his father, which was one of the most difficult decisions of her life. But she felt God's calling and attempted to join the Maryknoll Sisters but was denied because she was too old as well as divorced twice.

An idea grew in her head, however. She decided to become an independent sister at the prison. She traveled to Our Lady of the Assumption Church in Ventura and, alone there, announced her own private vows of service, chastity, and fidelity.

Shortly after taking her vows, she moved into the prison. The first few months, she stayed in a bunk bed among the women but later moved into her own cell that held a crucifix, a cot, a Bible, and an English-to-Spanish dictionary.

One story recounted in the book *Prison Angel* occurred early on in her stay after a rapist was severely beaten into unconsciousness by other inmates. Mother Antonia washed his wounds and attempted to say the Hail Mary in Spanish. A guard informed her that the man was a rapist and deserved the brutal beating he'd received. When she attempted to continue with the prayer, she got stuck, unsure of her Spanish, but the beaten man came to and finished the prayer for her.

The guard was so moved that he helped Mother Antonia carry him to a bed and helped with the man's wounds. She knew then that having the guards see the inmates as people worthy of respect and yes, even love, would be one of her main goals.

Mother Antonia worked for years to improve the prison but also worked with the prisoners to seek forgiveness for what they had done and to offer forgiveness to those who had wronged them. She knew that one of the main causes of violence was lacking forgiveness. In one reported instance she pleaded and begged a man to forgive a relative's murderer because she knew that if he did not, there would surely be more violence. The man forgave.

By 1997, others had heard of the work she was doing and offered to help. Some even wanted to join her. And thus was born the Eudist Servants of the Eleventh Hour, which was approved by the bishop of Tijuana, giving older women an avenue in which to dedicate their lives to a religious purpose and work with the poor. The order is typically open to women aged forty-five to sixty-five. Just a few years ago, there were up to nineteen sisters, most of whom worked in the prison.

Mother Antonia often visited her seven surviving children, James, Kathleen, Theresa, Carol, Tom, Elizabeth, and Anthony; more than forty-five grandchildren; and a growing number of great-grandchildren. They called her the Eveready Battery because she just kept going.

In 2013, Mother Antonia passed away at the age of eighty-six. In all, Mother Antonia spent more than thirty years living in a cell where she said she found true freedom. In the dark prison to which she brought so much light.

Discussion Questions

1. What aspect of Mother Antonia's calling or story made the biggest impression on you?

2. Have you ever stepped outside your comfort zone to serve God? What do you think stops most people from stepping out as Mother Antonia did?

3. Mother Antonia had grown children and grandchildren—she became a religious much later in life. How do you think her age helped her to fulfill her mission? Is there ever a time when we are too old to serve God?

CHAPTER FIVE

The Medical Mission
Philip Hawley Jr.

Then he said to his disciples, "The harvest is plentiful, but
the laborers are few; therefore ask the Lord of the harvest
to send out laborers into his harvest."

—Matthew 9:37–38

After a trip to Africa to attend a Marian conference in
1954, Monsignor Anthony Brouwers, the director of the
Propagation of the Faith in Los Angeles, wanted to know
what could be done to help the needy there.

Asking for Catholics to provide training and leadership in schools
and hospitals throughout Africa, he created the Lay Mission-
Helpers Association in 1955 and the Mission Doctors Association
in 1959 to do precisely that. The two organizations serve in thirty-
six countries; its members have offered a combined total of more
than two thousand years of service.

Elise Fredericks, who has been involved with the organization
for thirty-five years, explains that she is moved on a daily basis
about the work that's being done. "We don't send people to pros-
elytize, but we send them to witness to their own faith."

I ask her about the bravery of those who travel to underdeveloped countries, and she jokes that they're not so much brave as
"abnormally optimistic."

"It's what we're supposed to do," she says. "It's not supposed to be easy."

This is a story about a "not very easy" missionary trip by Dr. Phillip Hawley Jr. Elise recounted the story to me, knowing that her friend would be reluctant to talk about these mission trips himself. "Humility is his middle name," she says, joking that she can't send him out to fundraise because he belittles everything he does. "I tell him all the time he's got to toot his own horn a little bit," she laughs. "Getting Phil to tell me the story was difficult, but finally he relented. It starts out fittingly on a road some call 'the Road of Death.'"

• • •

It was raining when they set out for El Camino de la Muerte (The Road of Death) high up in the Andes Mountains in Bolivia. A bad sign.

Dr. Philip Hawley Jr. stepped on to the "open-air bus"—actually an old truck with seats, a rusted tin roof, and no windows. Heading up into the towering Andes Mountains, it was the best they were going to get.

The team Dr. Philip was with consisted of two doctors, six nurses, and a pharmacist. They were heading high up in the Andes to provide medical care for people in the remotest, most inaccessible villages. Dr. Philip was there on behalf of the Mission Doctors Association, which has trained, sent, and supported Catholic doctors and sometimes even their families serving people of all faiths in some of the most underserved areas of the world.

They would be traveling eight thousand feet up a narrow, one-lane road high up into the Andes. It might be too kind to call it a road. It's actually just mud, typically a single lane wide, created by earth movers digging a few feet at a time into the mountain. Hundreds reportedly die on this road each year, a reality made all too clear by the presence of several stone altars and crosses on the roadside commemorating loved ones lost.

The jungle roads are treacherous, with little room for maneuvering. Just that day, the medical missionaries heard of an accident a few miles ahead. The road had collapsed under the weight of the rain, sending a bus full of people over the edge, plunging thousands of feet to their deaths.

Dr. Philip got on the bus anyway. But it's not about courage, he insists. "It's more of a self-serving thing," he laughs. "I do this to get closer to God. I'm not knowingly stepping into the vortex of doom."

No. Just El Camino de la Muerte.

Philip sat on the right side of the bus, crammed in by medical supplies. The bus traveled slowly over the extremely narrow and rain-soaked road, soon reaching an elevation of about five thousand feet. Soon, they reached a hairpin turn covered in seventy feet of rushing water. The water crashed down the jungle-covered mountain like a river, funneled into the tiny road, and poured out into the jungle thousands of feet below. But because it moved so fast, it was impossible to tell how deep it was.

There was no way to turn around, so the bus driver decided to push through. "It became clear very quickly that this wasn't a good idea," says Philip.

The driver hugged the hillside, but the bus immediately lost traction and slipped closer to the edge. In an act of reflex or desperation, the driver gunned the engine. But the spinning wheels beneath the bus immediately lost all traction, and the bus slipped even further toward the edge. And they weren't stopping.

Philip was on the side of the bus facing the cliff, so he clearly saw the outer tire slip over the edge as he looked down at the jungle, thousands of feet below. A few others jumped out of the bus and were hanging onto the vehicle's left side. They dared not abandon the vehicle altogether because, alone, they would immediately be swept off the side of the mountain by the torrent of water. So they clung on desperately.

For a moment Philip considered joining them, but he was trapped by stacks of medical supplies on his left. At just that moment the driver once again gunned the engine, and the bus teetered on the edge as the water barraged the side of the vehicle, wearing away the road a little more with each passing second.

He says that's when it hit him. "I may die."

He expected the realization to be accompanied by panic. But something else happened. "All the anxiety I felt turned into a quiet calm," he says. "There was a quiet sadness, but the fear was completely gone."

His mind immediately went to his family, to his daughter who would be getting married in two months. "She always talked about how wonderful it would be for me to walk her down the aisle," he says. "I wanted to walk her down the aisle. But at that moment, I thought, apparently I'm not going to be able to."

The bus slipped even more, close to going over the edge. "It felt like time stopped," he says. He was aware of a great commotion and yelling, but for him, the world went silent. He reflected on his wonderful family, his wonderful life. As the bus teetered on the brink of a steep cliff, he could feel only...gratitude.

At just that moment, the driver slammed the bus into reverse and the wheels somehow caught a patch of earth. The bus rocked severely toward and then away from the cliff and finally retreated from the landslide.

After a few hours, the rains finally stopped. The team simply continued on their mission to help those in need of medical care. "It all ended happily. I got to walk my daughter down the aisle," he says.

• • •

Dr. Philip has been doing mission trips since 1979. His first missionary trip was to a polio clinic in Mexico, where young children rode in on burros. Thankfully, the scourge of polio has almost disappeared. But since then, he's been to Guatemala, the Peruvian Amazon, and Ecuador numerous times.

"When I started, I honestly didn't know why I wanted to do it," he says. "It was a calling I didn't recognize as a calling, but the Holy Spirit infused in me some desire."

After graduating from the University of Notre Dame and USC Medical School, he completed his training in general pediatrics at Los Angeles Children's Hospital. He also served as an assistant professor of clinical pediatrics at the University of Southern California School of Medicine and was a board member of Mission Doctors Association, where he worked behind the scenes for many years. When his two children were old enough, he felt called to return to active missionary work.

"When I returned to the field in 2000 I could see that the call to do this work was profound and loud," he says. "It was something that I needed to do, and I was able to do it." So every year, the successful doctor/father/professor was inspired by his faith to travel to some places that could only be reached by machete, open bus, or foot.

Dr. Philip takes his work very seriously but not himself. One can hardly get him to talk about himself at all. He looks exactly how you'd hope your pediatrician would look. Graying hair, alert eyes, trim and fit. He's also one of the funniest people you'll meet. Ask him about his medical mission trips to South America, and he has numerous amusing stories, like this one:

Jungle medicine is a lot different from what I do at Children's Hospital, starting with daily wake-up call from this wretched rooster. He must have been born in a different time zone because he starts crowing at about 2:30 every morning. He lives less than ten feet from my cabin, and he is the cause of many murderous thoughts I've had in the past few weeks. I even invented new cuss words for this foul animal. It doesn't seem fair that I'm so often tempted to sin while I'm in the jungle trying to repent for my many past sins. I think I'm digging a deeper hole, if that's possible.

I've been to several remote sites, but none quite as unique as this one in the Amazon. We have a fully staffed hospital located on a river, hundreds of miles from the closest road—meaning every supply comes by boat or, more accurately, a canoe. Resources are scarce in a way that I could never imagine before coming here. We can only keep the electricity running a few hours each morning, and then another few hours each evening—and there's always the chance that we'll run out of fuel or the generator won't fire up. Of course, emergencies don't happen when it's convenient, so when I need an emergency lab, I often have to do without because there is no electricity. Or a patient lands on our doorstep at 2:00 AM, and the only light I have to work from is an old kerosene lamp.

We have just nine simple lab tests available here (as compared to tens of thousands in the US). Something as simple as an electrolyte panel or a bacterial culture is not available, so when treating an infection, I have to take my best guess. We have no X-ray machine, but we have an ultrasound that we use mostly for obstetrical and surgical emergencies. It's an eclectic assortment of equipment, and the utterly amazing staff of people here work to great advantage for the tens of thousands of mostly indigenous people living in the Rio Napo region of the Peruvian Amazon.

A few nights ago, a patient's blood pressure was dangerously low, and he was not responding to the IV fluids we were giving him. We found some dopamine in the pharmacy (a dangerous drug in the best of circumstances, which this wasn't), but I sat down and did the calculations for an IV dopamine drip. This is one of those things that perhaps only a doctor or nurse will appreciate—dopamine is a medication that is almost always give through a fancy so-called central IV line close to a patient's heart (we have none of those), and it is given through a precise electrical pump (nope, none of those either), and given while an array of high-tech monitors provide moment-to-moment data about the patient's heart and lung function (here we use fifty-year-old manual blood pressure cuffs and our eyes and hands).

So there I am, late at night in this darkened hospital ward, doing my calculations on a piece of paper that had already been used twice before but had enough blank space that it was placed in the "clean" paper tray. A pig walks past me and sniffs my leg while I'm trying to figure out the safest way to give dopamine without electrical IV pumps or monitoring equipment. I wag my leg at the pig to move him along, and he responds by snorting a disgusting (and enormous) clot of phlegm on my scrub pants. I cursed—again—and then turned my attention back to the patient.

The story ended happily for everyone but the pig. We had pork for dinner that night.

When asked about his work in Ecuador, he jokes about remembering an elderly patient that grabbed his face, rubbed his head, kissed him repeatedly, and then asked for parasite medicine because she had been vomiting worms for the past few weeks.

Those are the stories he tells. But when you ask him why he goes on his mission trips, he becomes serious. When Dr. Hawley was preparing for his first mission trip as a member of Mission Doctors Association, he spent a great deal of time studying the culture of the people he would serve, and the diseases prevalent in those faraway jungles.

But he soon came to realize that studying medical journals and books wouldn't help him as much as he'd hoped. "I realize that this work has no more to do with exotic cultures than the Gospel of Christ has to do with the font style used in its printing," he says. "It has no more to do with tropical diseases than my Catholic Bible has to do with the cow that donated its hide for the cover."

"I realize that our work as Catholic missionary doctors is not really about bringing modern medicine to the 'jungle.' It is not about curing disease, though we may occasionally do so," he says. "Our work is about relieving suffering, and often for just a few hours or a few days."

He says that was a difficult lesson to learn for a physician. "Gradually, I have learned that the people I serve are not really starving for more medicine…. They are starving for a more profound form of healing. They are starving for Christ's love—just as I am."

He says he came to understand that "the medical details" of his work are important "only if I show to my patients the love of Jesus. In most cases, my work as a physician will have only a fleeting effect, and sometimes none at all," he says. "I must reflect Jesus's love, or I have done nothing of consequence."

As a mission doctor, he feels he is called "to reveal the love of Christ." He often quotes Mother Teresa: "'It's not how much we give but how much love we put into giving.' This is why the Catholic element of Mission Doctors Association is so important. Ultimately, it is the one gift we offer that has lasting importance," he says. "Medicine is a perfect vessel for our mission, but it is not our ultimate mission."

Philip has practiced pediatrics for years in California. His life is not about him. He believes that's the most important lesson he's learned. In fact, when he learned his daughter was sick, he knew he had to deal with it without bothering her about his own emotions. So he sat down to write a journal. But instead of writing about his own feelings, he instead ended up writing a thriller about an emergency room doctor who travels to South America to uncover a violent web of deceit. The book became a bestseller. After his daughter had recovered, Philip went on a book tour and was signed to a multi-book deal by a major publisher. But he knew that as much as he'd love to write novels, his true love was helping others through medicine and spreading the message of Christ's love. He turned away the major book deal.

Instead, Philip watches his granddaughter as often as possible and volunteers at a local Catholic hospice. And still working with the Mission Doctors Association, he travels to distant unseen villages in South America delivering much needed medical care and the message of the Gospel. He might not still sit on the cliff side of the bus, but he'll be the doctor on the bus praying, smiling, and full of gratitude.

Discussion Questions

1. Dr. Hawley often uses humor to describe what he does. Is that an effective form of evangelization?
2. How can you incorporate your work with spreading the Gospel? What mission has God entrusted to you?
3. Dr. Hawley decided to set aside his writing career in order to dedicate his time to medical missions. Do you think you would have made the same choice? Why or why not?

CHAPTER SIX

Love for the Win
Lauren Hill

I give you a new commandment, that you love one another.
Just as I have loved you, you also should love one another.

—John 13:34

It was a layup. Nothing easier in the world, right? And nothing more difficult.

It wasn't the final shot of an NBA finals. It wasn't a Cinderella college team earning a berth in the Sweet Sixteen. It was so much more important than that. We all watched. And we were inspired.

We watched a little blonde girl play a game she loved. She wasn't as fast as she used to be. She had pain. But she played. And she scored a left-handed layup because her right arm didn't really work anymore.

It was a game specifically scheduled for her. But in the end, it was a game played for others. Lauren Hill was diagnosed with diffuse intrinsic pontine glioma (DIPG) her senior year of high school. It is a terminal disease. She knew it. Confused as to what God's plan could be, Lauren asked God what he wanted from her.

"One January night, I was having a meltdown," Lauren told one columnist. "I asked God if I could do anything. I didn't know what He sent me here for. I wanted to know what He sent me here for. Whatever you sent me here for, I'm ready to do."

Her story bears a striking contrast with that of a young woman named Brittany Maynard, twenty-nine, who, around the same time, was diagnosed with a stage-4 glioblastoma and quickly became the public face of the right-to-die movement when she announced in a YouTube video that she would commit suicide when the pain became too great. In November of 2014, she ended her own life at her home in Portland, Oregon.

She wrote a note that said, among other things, "Good-bye world. Spread good energy. Pay it forward!"

Lauren, however, came to understand that her life could still be a gift to others. She came to understand that through the attention on her, she might be able to do some good for other children diagnosed with DIPG.

"What keeps me going is remembering why I'm here," she said.

The young woman, who some days couldn't balance herself, who couldn't walk or swallow on other days, and who felt pain so bad all she could do was close her eyes and pray for it to pass, said the hardest part was watching her family suffer. She said she prayed for them because she knew that their suffering would continue after her life here was over.

Lauren Hill knew she was dying, but she chose to live. She chose to live for her family. She chose to attend college. She chose to play basketball, a game that she'd loved since she was old enough to dribble a ball. And she played it to help children she would never meet.

Lauren loved playing basketball, and when she was diagnosed with brain cancer in her senior year of high school, she still continued with her plans to play basketball at Mount St. Joseph University. Her prognosis, however, was grim.

• • •

Mount St. Joseph University's head basketball coach, Dan Benjamin, said that the doctors thought Lauren would make it to

Christmas, but not much more. Unfortunately, that was before the university's scheduled first game against Hiram. So the Catholic university petitioned the NCAA to allow them to open the season early so that Lauren could achieve her dream of actually playing collegiate basketball.

Soon, news of Lauren and the game began spreading, and so many wanted to be a part of this extraordinary event and this inspiring young woman's efforts that the little Catholic university was forced to move the game to the ten-thousand-seat arena at nearby Xavier University. The game between Mount St. Joseph and Hiram sold out within an hour.

Nobody could remember another time when a women's game at Mount St. Joseph sold out. ESPN was there. Hundreds of media outlets. And with the world watching, Hill scored a left-handed layup to open the game. The country watched and cheered her on.

Benjamin reportedly said, "What I'll never forget about the game at the Cintas Center is the way they made something remarkable happen for one afternoon that meant the world to somebody. The execution of the first play will stick with me, the many practices of what we called Lauren's layup. That was her play. For her to go out and make it on the first attempt was amazing. I watch it by myself all the time and I go crazy."

WNBA great Elena Delle Donne attended the game and reportedly said,

> When I first heard Lauren's story I was moved by her courage and perspective on life. Immediately I knew I wanted to witness her dream come true. What the 10,000 plus crowd and I experienced on Sunday was something I couldn't have even imagined. It was the Lauren Hill effect. She had the ability to touch every person in that building and leave a lasting impact on all of our lives. Watching her accomplish her dream with a huge smile on her face while

battling constant pain and weakness showed everyone in that building, and across the country, just how strong Lauren truly is. The roar of the crowd when she made her first and last lay-up of the game is something that I cannot describe with words but I can still close my eyes and replay it in my head....

Lauren may not be able to beat this illness right now, but because of her courageous voice and infectious smile, her legacy will live on to fight this horrible disease so one day there is a cure. Anyone who sees her story, or is lucky enough to be in the same building as Lauren, is instantly touched and moved to do something. I feel truly blessed to have been in her presence on Sunday.

LeBron James tweeted a message to Lauren, saying, "You are simply and truly 'AMAZING' Lauren Hill!!! Thank you for inspiring me and I'll try my best to match you! Congrats on your game. Also be looking out for a package from I to You! You're Awesome!!!" He sent her an autographed pair of sneakers in the mail.

She joked to one writer that the shoes didn't fit.

When asked what she wanted her legacy to be, she said,

Last January, I said to God I'll do anything to be a voice for this cancer and all the kids that can't speak their symptoms. Parents are left baffled, because they don't know what's wrong with their kids. [Kids] can't express what's happening to them. I prayed I'd be the voice and that I'd do anything that gave me an opportunity to raise awareness and raise research money.... That was a couple months after diagnosis. The first couple months I was angry. Why does this happen to me? Why does it happen to anybody? I believe God has the last say. And I feel like I've accomplished what I intended.... My values have switched around. My dad asked me what I wanted for Christmas. No material item matters to me. I just want to spend time with my family.

Lauren Hill died on April 10, 2015. She was nineteen.

"God has a new game plan for Lauren Hill," said Tony Aretz, president of Mount St. Joseph University in a statement. "Her light will continue to shine on us all as her supporters worldwide continue her mission of increasing awareness and finding a cure for DIPG.... We are forever grateful to have had Lauren grace our campus with her smile and determined spirit. She has left a powerful legacy. She taught us that every day is a blessing; every moment a gift."

Lauren once reportedly said, "If I do pass, I don't want people to say I lost. I want them to say, 'She kicked DIPG's butt and raised a lot of money for research.'... By the end of the year, [we] want to raise a million dollars. That'd be really awesome. That'd be the best Christmas present."

The Cure Starts Now reports that Hill's efforts raised $1.5 million for research on DIPG.

What more can be said? Under the most difficult and tragic of circumstances, Lauren Hill trusted God and lived for others. And oh yeah, she kicked DIPG's butt and raised a lot of money for research.

Discussion Questions

1. Have you ever had to put all your faith in God even though things in your life seemed to be going wrong?
2. As you think about the two dying women in this story—Lauren and Brittany—what strikes you about the way they chose to face their circumstances? What do you think you would say, if a friend faced a similar situation?
3. The move to legalize assisted suicide in the US has grown stronger, with several states, including Oregon, Montana, Washington, Vermont, and California, passing laws related to this issue. What can Christians do to promote the sanctity of life?

CHAPTER SEVEN

A Home of Hope

Dr. George Isajiw

I call heaven and earth to witness against you today that
I have set before you life and death, blessings and curses.
Choose life so that you and your descendants may live,
loving the LORD your God, obeying him, and holding fast
to him; for that means life.

—Deuteronomy 30:19

This is a story that involves two buildings. The first was
a beautiful three-story, stucco-coated Baptist seminary
with grand pillars guarding the front entrance. Its architecture is as impressive as its history. Each of the three pavilions
were topped by a gabled roof and cupola, with the largest cupola
standing proudly, almost boastfully, on the central pavilion. In this
very building just outside of Philadelphia, Dr. Martin Luther King
Jr. was educated and achieved his bachelor of divinity degree.

Years later, the building was transformed into a medical building
in which the library became an abortion clinic.

The other building in this story is an abandoned convent on the
grounds of a Catholic parish in Philadelphia which nobody seemed
to want after the Servants of the Immaculate Heart of Mary moved
out. Its architecture is nothing to boast of. It was added onto and
moved from one corner of the property to the other, and finally it

was left empty until it was transformed into a home for women with crisis pregnancies.

Dr. George Isajiw spent many days standing outside the former seminary which housed the abortion clinic in rain, snow, and freezing temperatures in a white doctor's coat and glasses too large for his face. Dr. Isajiw would speak to the women outside the clinic as they neared the entrance. He is not an eloquent man or given to hyperbole. He is a kind and quiet man comfortable with facts. He would calmly explain to the women or the couples heading in to the clinic the developmental stages of a fetus in the womb using plastic models. But he wasn't lecturing or shaming. He offered them help. He asked what they needed. And for many, it was the first time they could remember when somebody had cared enough to ask. If, however, they continued to walk in, he would silently pray.

He prayed a lot.

Dr. Isajiw wore his white doctor's coat in front of the abortion clinic because it was easier to get people's attention identifying as a physician, rather than just a sidewalk counselor, especially a male one.

Workers inside the clinic would attempt to dismiss Dr. Isajiw and imply to the women who entered the clinic that Dr. Isajiw wasn't a doctor at all. They'd say that he was just "dressed as a doctor."

One of the doctors who stood inside the clinic, impeccably dressed in a three-piece suit, bore a stark contrast to Dr. Isajiw. The abortionist was tall, youthful looking, robust, and married to a fashion model. He was successful by all counts, Dr. Marshall Klavan was head OB-GYN at Crozer-Chester Medical Center, where he was liked and respected by his associates.

The son of a poor Jewish grocer who escaped with his family from the genocidal clutches of Nazis in Lithuania, Dr. Marshall Klavan later became a sad historical footnote when, after attempting suicide in the late 1990s, he was resuscitated, kicking off one of the first and most infamous "wrongful life lawsuits" in which he sought the legal means to die. The courts stood against him, and he remained in a persistent vegetative state for years.

But that was years later.

So impressive was Dr. Isajiw's work outside the clinic that when PBS's *Frontline* did a documentary on abortion, they featured him in their "Alternatives to Abortion" segment. Many pro-lifers who have seen the 1983 documentary on the Internet say they can't believe that PBS would show such an impressive man because it made pro-lifers look good.

• • •

His compassionate faith is remarkable, yet Isajiw traces his convictions to his own grandfathers, who were both married priests in the Ukranian Catholic Rite. Dr. Isajiw never met his maternal grandfather, Fr. Nicholas Konrad, because he was born four years after the priest's martyrdom at the hands of communists in Ukraine after visiting a sick person. In fact, Fr. Konrad was beatified by the Catholic Church on June 27, 2001, by Pope John Paul II.

That strong faith was handed down to Dr. Isajiw. Always compassionate and willing to help women in crisis pregnancies, Dr. Isajiw would go so far as to offer them a place to stay. In the beginning of the conversation, he wouldn't explain that it would be living with his wife and six children in a solidly middle-class neighborhood.

But for some of the women, this was exactly what they needed in order to say yes to the growing life within them. Sometimes they stayed in a room with his daughters for months. He said that sometimes they became very close to his family and felt very much like part of the family. It was just one more seat around an already crowded oval-shaped dinner table.

"I've got to give credit to my wife, Patricia, who volunteered our home," said Isajiw. "She's the real hero." He admits there were many initial concerns about the extra burden on the family, both financially and practically, as well as the effect it may have on the children. But Patricia knew something about crisis pregnancies and understood all too well the plight of these mothers.

"Patricia herself had experienced a teenage pregnancy. She was seventeen when she placed the child for adoption. There was also a time in her own life when she accepted help from a family who was not related to her under difficult economic circumstances, long before we met and were married," he said. "So Patricia willingly accepted these mothers based on their immediate need and the pressure that they were experiencing for abortion within their own family and relationships with the father of the baby."

From 1981 to 1991, the Isajiws opened their home to care for twenty-eight homeless and pregnant women, sometimes three at a time. And many of the women would stay after their babies were born to give them time to get on their feet. Some of these women became very close to his daughters, he recalls. As a practicing physician and a father of six children, Dr. Isajiw never felt he was doing enough.

As a sidewalk counselor, Dr. Isajiw can remember a few times when a teenager admitted that she was being forced by her parents to have an abortion. He remembers leaving the clinic with them immediately and contacting a pro-life lawyer he knew, Mary Alice Duffy of Philadelphia, who then took emergency measures to obtain legal emancipation for similar teenagers so they could choose life.

In fact it was Duffy who, by some accounts, created the first all-female law firm in the country, along with a nurse named Jean Neary, who were at least partly responsible for inspiring Dr. Isajiw into the pro-life movement. Neary and Duffy had started a hotline called SOUL (Save Our Unborn Lives) in the early 1980s. By being listed in the phonebook, women interested in abortion might call the hotline, and Jean, who almost always answered the phone herself, would urge the women to carry the child and talk to them about what they needed.

Duffy asked Dr. Isajiw to testify in a Philadelphia court in defense of the hotline's right to list their phone number as an "abortion-related service" in the phone book after a pro-abortion group argued that this was false advertising. "Somehow she recruited me to testify on their behalf," he laughs.

He said he never believed the pro-abortion group had any grounds to stand on. He said that he thought their argument was ridiculous in that counseling for alcoholics didn't give people alcohol but would still properly be labeled alcohol counseling.

After testifying, he could've said he'd done enough, but his strong Catholic convictions urged him forward. He now says, "Their work convinced me of the need for pro-life physicians to take the lead in providing counseling for abortion-minded women." He felt called to do more. The late Dr. Joseph Gambescia, who Dr. Isajiw calls "the most important mentor in [his] professional life," asked for the blessing of Cardinal Krol, who gave him the "go ahead" to proceed with the Women's Pregnancy Health Services, providing a hotline for women in a crisis pregnancy.

He was then faced with women desperate for care calling his office. He could have said he was doing all he could do, but his faith once again demanded more of him.

As the number of callers to his office increased, Dr. Isajiw knew he couldn't possibly take any more women into his home, so he convinced ten other families to begin taking in women with crisis pregnancies who needed help in the Philadelphia area. Soon, this network of friends were receiving more referrals than they, too, could possibly accommodate.

Dr. Isajiw frequently came to moments when he was asked to do more than he even believed he and his family could do.

After many years of pro-life work, in 1986, some people assumed that we were involved in arranging adoptions—which, of course, we were not—but referred either to Catholic Social Services are some trusted pro-life attorneys. We received a call that a woman had given birth to a boy with multiple birth defects and wanted to place him for adoption. We passed this information on to the pro-life community, and several couples who were childless, went to see him in the hospital, considering adoption. They were all overwhelmed with seeing a low birth weight child on life support machinery, and felt they were not able to handle such a situation—perfectly understandable for young childless couples.

At around the same time we attended a lecture by the late Dr. Herbert Ratner of Chicago, who, a convert to the Catholic faith, was an expert on family relations (he used to publish the *Child and Family* magazine). The theme of that lecture was that the best gift that one could give your children was a brother or a sister! We both came to the conclusion simultaneously, that the Lord was asking us to adopt Andrew, especially since we were comfortable with his medical conditions and that otherwise he would have been put into the foster care system. We already had six children and our youngest was nine years old.

The family turned the living room into both a play area and a hospital room for the extremely sick child. They loved and nurtured Andrew through twelve surgeries in his short life of two years. Dr. Isajiw still calls Andrew a "God sent Blessing not only for Pat and I, but for the entire family!"

Helen McBlain remembers the child's funeral. "It was so very sad. But it was also joyous because we all knew that this child knew and loved a dad and a mom," she adds. "Andrew was loved."

It became very clear to Dr. Isajiw that the needs of these young women were not being met and that many of them needed more help than he or those shepherding families could offer, including issues of addiction, mental illness, and HIV on top of their crisis pregnancies. Instead of throwing his hands up and declaring he'd done enough, Dr. Isajiw once again sought to do more.

He'd heard that a group of nuns had recently vacated a fifty-four room, three-story stone convent on the campus of the Blessed Virgin Mary parish in Darby, Pennsylvania. He suggested using it as a shelter for women. He approached Monsignor Francis Schmidt, who was then pastor of the parish, and he said he would be very happy to lease the property for a home for women in need.

It is a sad irony that the abortion clinic in town had once been a seminary, and now this home for mothers with crisis pregnancies was being made from a convent. But renovating the building that was used for nuns into a home for pregnant mothers and newborn babies took some doing. "It took quite a few years," he said. "We all did some fundraising and with the grace of the good Lord we came up with Mothers' Home."

"I was never good at being in charge of anything so it really was the work of the Holy Spirit," he says in all seriousness. He credits the work of the Delaware County Pro-Life Coalition and the invaluable work of the Delaware County Lawyers for Life and the spiritual guidance of Fr. John McFadden.

Isajiw and his network of friends were able to raise the funds necessary to secure not only the site but skilled staff. The basement of the building that came to be known as "Mothers' Home" was converted to a community outreach center, which became their "Sharing Space." Finally, the first group of mothers moved in to the old convent in 1993.

Since then, Mothers' Home has housed over a thousand homeless pregnant women. Mothers' Home has offered women care, advice, a place to live, training, and counseling. Dr. Isajiw offered love to people who may have forgotten what that was. At present, twenty-eight young women at a time can live at Mothers' Home. They all participate in free daily classes on life skills, nutrition, parenting, labor and delivery, early infant care, housing, fertility awareness, and budgeting. There are occasional legal clinics addressing domestic abuse. Residents are required to perform ten hours of community service each month. These service hours are usually performed in the Sharing Space, where clothing and items are made available to the community. Case management is provided to assist residents to define and obtain their personal goals.

A typical resident usually remains at Mothers' Home for six months after the delivery of their babies. The popular Step-Up Program allows for four mothers to stay an additional twelve months at very low rent in two recently renovated apartments located in the building.

Helen McBlain recently spoke about one resident who had fled from war-torn Sierra Leone and is currently pursuing a degree at Neumann University with her heart set on becoming a doctor. Another woman was being pressured by her family to have an abortion but is now adamant about wanting to give her unborn child a chance at life.

One of the things that Dr. Isajiw takes great joy in is receiving letters, calls, or visits from former residents and hearing about them and the lives of their children. They often want to thank him, but he simply asks about them. He wants to hear how they're doing. Then he asks if there's anything he can do for them.

Discussion Questions

1. How does the sanctity of life affect the way you live?
2. How have you experienced children as a gift from God?
3. What does this story have to say about what it means to be pro-life?

CHAPTER EIGHT

"Save My School"
Tommy Geromichalos

He said to me, "This is the word of the LORD to
Zerubbabel: Not by might, nor by power, but by my spirit,
says the LORD of hosts.

—Zechariah 4:6

The Archdiocese of Philadelphia has closed down many
Catholic schools in recent years due to shifting demo-
graphics, including the elementary school my five children
attend. But we were far from alone.

I was searching around the Internet to find out about all the
different school closings when I came upon news that St. Cyril
school in Lansdowne, which had been recommended for closure
by the archdiocesan Blue Ribbon commission, was now remaining
open as a mission school.

I saw the news and couldn't help but smile. There's a story behind
the news story. And it's a great one. It happened just a few years
ago. If you put this story in a movie, nobody would believe it. Too
corny, they'd say. Way too Frank Capra.

This is a story about community. The kind of community that
many didn't think still exists in America, the kind that still believe
in wishes and miracles. But mostly this is a story about a little boy
who refused to give up on a miracle. When told what he wanted
was impossible, he believed the way only twelve-year-olds can.

• • •

Six years ago, Tommy Geromichalos was a twelve-year-old boy from Philadelphia who had a serious form of cystic fibrosis (CF). Tommy's sister had CF, too. When the Make-A-Wish Foundation approached his sister Samantha, she wished to meet Celine Dion.

When they asked Tommy what he wished for, he gave an answer they didn't expect. Tommy didn't want to meet a celebrity. He didn't want to play basketball against an NBA hero.

His wish was simple: "Save my school."

The Archdiocese of Philadelphia was closing Tommy's elementary school. Much of the Catholic population had moved into the suburbs, and the urban neighborhood just couldn't support the school anymore. Here's the letter Tommy wrote:

> My name is Tommy. I am 12 years old and I have Cystic Fibrosis. I have a special EMERGENCY WISH that I hope can come true. You guys are my last hope.
>
> My wish is to keep my school open until I graduate 8th grade. I go to St. Cyril of Alexandria School in East Lansdowne, PA. I'm in 6th grade. The Archdiocese plans to close my school. I know they don't want to but they think it would be best...but they just don't understand that my school is my second home and all the people there are my family.
>
> On October 31st, my Aunt Lorrie died of leukemia and cancer. She graduated from St. Cyril's in the 1950's, so did my Aunt Marcella and my other relatives including my sister Samantha, she is 15 and she has CF too. I am the last one in my family to go to St. Cyril's. All my life I have waited to be on the 3rd floor, that's where the 6th 7th and 8th graders are. Everyone knows that Miss Cashwell is the best 8th grade teacher in the world. When I am in 8th grade I will have the chance to have fun and learn. It's a tradition at St. Cyril's that 8th grade goes to Washington D.C. and all the 8th grade

Altar servers get to go to Dorney Park. We also have the best I.H.M. Sisters you will ever find in any school.

Sometimes reading is hard for me because have Dyslexia but I have the best teacher named. S. Ann. She has taught me and all my buddies since we were in 1st grade. We are a team and she wants to stick with us and help until we graduate. S. Ann has always been there for me and my family even when I was in the hospital.

I don't' make CF a big part of my life because, I just want to be a normal kid but sometimes it's just too hard. I've been in the hospital for C.F. with IV's in my arm and I've had surgeries on my stomach and my polyps. One time when I went in the hospital I even cried because I was afraid that God didn't love me. I asked my Mom, "How can God love me if he makes me suffer?" My mom cried and told me God loves all of us and some things happen for reasons we don't know about. Father Kearns came to visit me at St. Chris and he talked to me and I got my faith back again.

I don't' know how to save my school and I need your help. I'll do anything that can make a difference. We need a MIRACLE. Please help me convince Cardinal Rigali to keep my school open. My faith is strong because I go to a Catholic School. The spirit of St. Cyril is alive in me and everyone else who has been a part of St. Cyril School.

Please help me save my school. This is my Christmas Make A Wish.

Make-A-Wish executive director Dennis Heron said his request "blew us away." But after researching the issue and contacting the archdiocese, they came up against a cold hard reality. It cost $175,000 to run the school each year, and the money just wasn't there. There was no way they could do it.

Tommy's mother, Connie, who was a librarian at the school, told her son it was a "no-win situation." It just wasn't in anyone's power to fulfill his wish. She warned him that if he didn't change his wish, he likely wouldn't get another one. But Tommy insisted that he had no other wish.

Pastor Kearns also advised Tommy to change his wish. Although the priest also wanted the school to remain open, he told the boy, "There is a limit to what can be done."

Tommy wouldn't change his wish.

• • •

The school announced it was closing. But here comes the fun part.

A waitress at a bar told a local newspaper columnist about Tommy's story, and he wrote a column. Soon, other newspapers and television stations ran the story about Tommy's letter. The St. Cyril's community and the entire city was moved by the young boy's wish.

Soon, there was a committee hosting beef-and-beer fundraisers, a dance-athon, a pizza sale, a charity basketball tournament, and car washes. "I Believe" T-Shirts were sold. A local Dodge dealer even donated a car for a raffle. Alumni of the school came to fundraisers and met old friends they hadn't seen in years despite perhaps living within a mile of each other. The community was brought together.

By the end of March, the $200,000 "Save our School" goal was met and surpassed. Then Cardinal Justin Rigali paid a visit to the school and surprised everyone by announcing that the school was off the chopping block. Tommy had saved the school.

Tommy graduated from St. Cyril's. In fact, he graduated from Monsignor Bonner High School and went off to college. And this kid...well, young man, showed up at the newspaper to thank the columnist and the editors of the paper for all they'd done for him. *He* thanked them.

That's the kind of thing that just makes you think Catholic schools are doing something right after all.

DISCUSSION QUESTIONS

1. Sometimes children show wisdom beyond their years? Can you think of a time when a child had something to teach you?
2. Tommy was brave enough to ask for help. Do you find it harder to ask for help or to offer it?
3. What Catholic parents do you know whose faith has been tested as they've done their best to meet their children's educational needs?

CHAPTER NINE

The Unexpected Miracle

Meghan Johnson

Trust in the LORD with all your heart,
and do not rely on your own insight.

—Proverbs 3:5

Meghan Johnson doesn't know if she remembers the first time she saw little Ricky brought in. But we rarely take note of the biggest moments of our lives, those moments that will change everything. Meghan was a twenty-five-year-old blonde nurse working in the neonatal intensive care unit. She didn't know her life would change that day, but throughout everything that happened, she always kept her faith in God.

It is funny, though, how those big days in our lives sneak up on us like a sudden knock on the door. If we all knew those moments were coming, perhaps we'd respond better all the time. Someone just comes through a door and everything changes. In this case, little Ricky was wheeled through the doors of the NICU.

"He was my patient that night," Meghan remembers. She doesn't remember if it was the first time she saw him brought in. But she does remember at that moment having the strong sense that her life would never be the same.

• • •

The delivery room in the hospital forty miles outside Reno was silent at 8:04 AM on October 2, 2004. The baby just delivered didn't cry. He didn't breathe.

Silence can be the scariest sound.

The doctor immediately began chest compressions—a dangerous thing to do on a grown person, never mind on a premature newborn who weighed just over three pounds.

Nobody knows why things like this happen. Was it drug abuse by the mother? Was it just chance? Nobody really knows for sure. But all the whys in the world don't mean a thing when a baby isn't breathing.

Doctors performed a full resuscitation effort on the tiny infant. After several minutes, the baby labored through his first breath. It seemed like every breath after that was a labor as well for the little baby who would be called Ricky. He was quickly placed on a ventilator, and due to all his complications, several hours later, a transport team from the larger St. Mary's Regional Medical Center arrived to bring Ricky to Reno, and plans were immediately made to perform his first surgery. Ricky had what doctors call duodenal atresia, a birth defect that causes the intestines to kink off, inhibiting motility. There were eight areas of atresia throughout Ricky's small intestine...the most anyone there had seen in an infant. Ricky was in constant pain.

Little Ricky's life was never easy. His birth mother, who did show up at the hospital for a month or two, eventually stopped coming. "Ricky became my primary patient," said Meghan. And the head nurses always put Meghan in Ricky's room. "He was there for so long. That's what really made us connect," she said. "His mom wasn't there very much. That's why I felt like I was stepping into a role."

When Ricky woke from his many surgeries, it was Meghan's smiling face he often woke to. And when he slept, Meghan watched over him in the dark. Silently praying. Gently checking his vitals. On one of those days, Meghan flippantly asked the social worker in charge of Ricky's case when she was going to be able to take Ricky home.

The social worker promptly replied back, "Get your foster care license."

And then the twenty-five-year-old nurse surprised everyone, including herself, because she did just that. Meghan took classes and within a few months obtained her foster care license. Well-meaning friends warned her she was crazy, she was setting herself up for heartbreak. Meghan knew it was true. Her life would be turned upside down, they told her. That's true, too, she thought.

But the simple truth is that *every* act of self-giving love turns the world upside down. It seems like that's the one thing the world is never prepared for. Anytime we choose to love, we invite heartbreak. Some refuse to love wholeheartedly because of this; they shy away and shun love, unwilling to risk getting hurt. And yet, the decision to love is the bravest decision. Meghan made the decision to love that little baby. About three months later, she drove away from St. Mary's with Ricky.

It was his first trip that wasn't in an ambulance.

"I remember being amazed at how easy the whole process had been—to obtain the huge responsibility of a child," she says. "And not just any child...this was Ricky!"

She simply placed Ricky in a car seat and walked out the door, put him in the car, and drove away. "He was free, just like that!" she remembers.

I was simply being blessed with the opportunity to help a little boy who had endured more pain in his first eight months than most of us will know in a lifetime. It seemed so unfair that Ricky should go on facing life's obstacles without a mother simply because the risk for personal turmoil was too great. I knew I could help him—for whatever time I was allowed to have him. I remember telling so many that I knew I was setting myself up to be hurt, one way or another... but what I also knew was that no matter what, eventually, I would be OK...Ricky may not.

Ricky's prognosis was always grim. But Meghan tried to convince herself that everything would be all right. Meghan not only had a nursing degree, but she read everything she could find on duodenal atresia. Meghan had confidence that with love, education, prayer, and perseverance she could pull Ricky through this terrible disease. She had the confidence that so many young people have that miracles come made to order when we want them and in the exact way we want them.

There was no doubt in my mind at the time of discharge from St. Mary's that I alone could fix this baby! I was confident in how to handle his medical needs, and even more confident in the power of love and stability. Prayer of course would be essential, but what he really needed was a floor to roll around on, a dog to lick him, and a mommy to carry him through each obstacle. Then, I was sure, he would eat. Not only would he eat, he would stand up on his legs, push up with his shoulders, and ultimately turn the healthiest shade of pink that a baby can radiate!

Confident in the power of love, Meghan prayed constantly for Ricky and used every bit of the medical knowledge she had to make his life better, more comfortable. In those months, Meghan lived for his smiles. Whether it was placing the Dancing Elmo beside him on the floor or just making funny noises at him, she delighted in his every giggle. And he smiled right back at her in that way that babies do, his eyes sparkling and his hands and feet waving around with excitement. To little Ricky, his mother's smile was the greatest gift in the world. And she felt the same about his.

Despite all the pain he endured, there was something irresistible about Ricky. The way he went cross-eyed and smiled that toothless smile as she kissed the pacifier into his mouth. Then, something even better: One day Ricky took the pacifier from her mouth with his hand and plopped it into his own mouth. She remembers the way he danced excitedly in the bed because he knew he'd done something extraordinary because Meghan was clapping and laughing. And then he did it again and got just as excited again. Because Meghan did, too.

Meghan's friends threw her a baby shower when she brought Ricky home. She thanked them for demonstrating once again that God is always faithful to provide strength when it is needed. Meghan leaned heavily on her parents as well, who babysat Ricky. They fell in love with him, too.

But despite careful and loving interventions by his doctors and therapists and loving patience of friends and family, Ricky struggled to gain weight and get off the total parenteral nutrition tube, which was his main source of nutrition but was slowly destroying his liver.

Meghan cared for and loved Ricky through over a dozen surgeries. But eventually he began having a hard time tolerating tube feedings and couldn't keep food down at all. Soon, he recoiled at the sight of food, knowing that it would cause him pain. This prompted a car trip to California, to Stanford Medical Center for evaluation and a possible surgical intervention. With Ricky in the car seat, Meghan drove mile after mile listening to the Christian song "He's My Son." Mark Schultz wrote this award-winning song for his own son, who was battling cancer. And yet the song poured out comfort and grace for Meghan as she offered the words of Mark's song as her own prayer.

Meghan remembers feeling a sense of anticipation and hope as she and Ricky made that long drive to the hospital in California.

"I couldn't help but feel some excitement and confidence in what God was going to bring out of this trip," she says. "Somehow, I just couldn't think of one reason why God wouldn't choose to heal Ricky. How could he not want this amazing little life to continue on and teach others about perseverance, strength, and trust?"

Meghan thought her love and her faith could save him. And if ever there was a woman who could have loved her child into living, it was Meghan. She believed God would take advantage of the opportunity to show the world his power by saving this smiling little boy. "How could God *not* take advantage of this opportunity?"

But things got worse. It turns out Ricky was not a candidate for the surgery. Doctors performed a simple surgery—a temporary fix—for Ricky and then suddenly, he began losing blood, dying in front of Meghan's eyes. The doctors ran tests and couldn't discover the source of the bleeding. Little Ricky's bandages became soaked with blood after a few minutes, and Meghan repeatedly reapplied new bandages.

Sitting by little Ricky's bedside, she questioned God. "Can you hear me? Am I getting through? Can you see this little boy?" She was desperate for answers. This wasn't the way the story was supposed to end for Ricky. He was too beautiful. And she and her parents loved him so very much. Somehow Ricky survived that first night despite losing half of his entire blood volume. When he awoke, he threatened many times to remove his breathing tube himself, and finally Ricky was given his way and the doctors took him off the ventilator. His transformation was almost instantaneous, and Meghan and her parents were so thrilled to have the alert and adorable little boy they all knew back. He was his smiling, wide-eyed self, and Meghan was convinced more than ever that Ricky would be a miracle.

"I was able to hold him for about ten minutes," Meghan says. "And then he promptly reached for his bed, just wanting to sleep."

At that moment they all hoped that those precious moments were a precursor to a miracle. Instead, they soon discovered, they were a gift. A final gift.

Meghan's father sat with Ricky while he slept as Meghan and her mother grabbed a quick lunch. But when she returned, she checked the dressing on his feeding tube. She was devastated to find dark red blood dripping out of the tubing. The dressing was saturated in a matter of minutes and for the second time in two days, he was bleeding out of control. The treatment routine that was performed the first time was begun again but not before the vomiting resumed as well, worse than before.

After more debate and consults with surgeons and GI doctors, the decision was made to remove the tube and replace it with one that would provide pressure to what they believed were large veins that developed in the tract where the feeding tube lay. Meghan requested that it be removed completely, as Ricky could be fed through a tube down his nose, but doctors did not feel they would be able to stop the bleeding.

The bleeding risk just in the removal of the tube was great, but Meghan felt there was no choice. They went ahead and placed the new tube, and the bleeding appeared to have stopped. However, the blood that remained in his stomach would still have to clear on its own.

She prayed for so many things that day and night. She prayed that his nutrition would move through his intestine or drain from the tube rather than cause him to vomit. But mostly she prayed for his pain to stop. "I can't begin to explain how difficult it is to watch him when this happens, and it just needs to stop," she said at the time.

And in the quiet of the night, she thanked God for those few last minutes with Ricky. "At first, I couldn't have been more confused or angry," she says. "Why should this precious little boy be forced to endure such incredible suffering time after time? Why should he pay the price for the mistakes of others for so long, and now be faced with a death that came with fear and pain?"

She stared at her little boy, lying so tired and weak on that hospital bed, and it suddenly dawned on her that God indeed had heard her. He was going to heal Ricky, not her way but by granting her little boy total release from his pain. "He had fought for so long, been stronger than any of us could have been, and it was finally time for his reward. He wasn't going to have to return to surgery with the possibility of dying on the white-covered tables he had grown to fear so much. He wasn't going to face the pain and discomfort of food moving through his intestines ever again. And he would not have to endure a grueling hospital stay for a transplant that likely would have extended his time here by five years at the most. He was going to peacefully slip away in the arms of those who loved him more than life itself."

Ricky was tired, and Meghan finally realized that God was saying, "You can rest."

In his final two hours, Ricky was peaceful and calm in Meghan's arms in the rocking chair. She felt love. Love in a measure she never thought she could feel. "What an honor to be a part of this little fighter's reward as he was carried away by his rescuer," she says. Just as Meghan had rescued Ricky and brought him home, so too did Christ look upon the little suffering boy and take him home.

Meghan knows Ricky's life was not in vain. "One single year and he made a greater impact on others than most will ever do," he says. "His life was not in vain, and his influence will carry on forever."

Life is never in vain when we love and are loved.

Meghan and her parents made little bookmarks for the funeral with the picture of Ricky and his story. On the way to the funeral in the car with her mother and father, they all panicked as Meghan's father realized that he had left one of the boxes of Ricky's bookmarks on top of the car. He quickly pulled over, and they all got out of the car and looked back to see them fluttering like wings all over Wilbur May Parkway.

The three of them ran around the road picking up as many bookmarks they could. The panic though quickly turned to amusement, and they all laughed while chasing down the bookmarks fluttering all around the highway. When they retrieved as many as they could, Meghan's father said they should get back to the car. They said of the remaining bookmarks that now even strangers would be touched by this child when they came across them.

In that moment of laughter, she thought of Ricky. Free from pain, smiling that toothless smile and curling his legs like a little toy. She had received her miracle, after all. True, there had been no earthly cure for his rare disease. The real miracle was that Ricky knew and gave love his whole life through. That's the real miracle and the most improbable one of them all.

Discussion Questions

1. Have you ever prayed to God for a miracle and been surprised by his response?
2. Have you ever put your heart out there and loved someone despite a terrible risk?
3. What is one thing you can do this week to reach out in a meaningful way to a parent who is struggling?

CHAPTER TEN

A Man and His Rosary

Mike Casey

But I trusted in your steadfast love;
my heart shall rejoice in your salvation.

—Psalm 13:5

When I first read about the story of the man who fought to say the rosary in his small town outside Boston, I immediately called him. Although distrustful of the media, he said he spoke to me only because the newspaper I write for, the *National Catholic Register*, was owned by EWTN. In conversing with him, what struck me is how trusting of God Mike Casey was. I admit that there are many times in my life where I struggle with accepting God's will for me. I have often thought of Mike Casey in those times and prayed for a similar calming faith.

Mike Casey is a praying man. The father of two believes in the power of prayer to change things. It's easy to believe in the power of prayer when you see how a little prayer can change so many things.

It all started simply. Mike Casey wanted to pray. As part of the America Needs Fatima movement, Mike wanted his town of Upton, Massachusetts, to join other groups across America in a Public Square Rosary Crusade.

The event was to be held on October 15, 2011, and would involve more than 7,500 groups nationwide. Casey could have prayed outside the rectory of a local church as they had the previous year. But this time Mike, a respected local businessman who owned a hardwood floor company, asked the town administrators, called "selectmen," if he and a group of others could pray the rosary in the town common. "Part of the rosary is penance, and praying in public is part of that," explained Mike.

The official told him they'd consider his request and not to bother coming to the town meeting. They would e-mail their decision to him. Well, Mike didn't exactly like the sound of that, so he went to the meeting anyway. And he couldn't believe what happened. "When my agenda item came up, all three of them unanimously denied my request," he said. "They said they didn't want to offend anyone in the town."

The selectmen were reportedly "uncomfortable" with the idea of public prayer. Selectman Ken Picard told a newspaper, "We weren't sure if having a prayer service on the common would be in line with [the separation of church and state]."

Mike was shocked. Then, when he wasn't allowed to speak, he left. Mike knew there was something wrong with their decision. But he wasn't going to fight it. He didn't want a battle. He didn't want a media circus. He didn't want lawyers. He just wanted to pray the rosary.

Mike scrambled around and quickly received permission to hold the rosary at the entrance of their new church. And he was just happy that he was able to pray the rosary that night along with thousands of others nationwide.

That might have been the end of it...until one of Mike's friends told him that the town shouldn't have denied his request. He told Mike he had constitutional rights, and Mike began to wonder if maybe Jesus wanted him to do something more.

• • •

A friend of his, Rita, sent a letter to the local *Town Crier*, which is distributed biweekly to all 5,700 addresses in Mendon and Upton.

Al Holman, the paper's publisher, read the letter and was moved enough to write an editorial:

> The response from the Selectmen was a simple "No" and the reason was given that they did not want to offend any taxpayers. I have read both the State Constitution and the Constitution of the United States and have yet to find where the right to assemble and free speech can be stopped by the possibility of offending taxpayers. The common is a public place and is owned by all the taxpayers and therefore is open to the public to assemble on. It should be noted that Upton has no by-law that requires a permit for public demonstrations or marches, and saying the Rosary would not seem to me an action that would incite a riot.

Well, it seems that the local paper has a number of out-of-town subscribers, one of which is *The Boston Herald*. A reporter at the *Herald*, Jessica Heslam, read Holman's piece and decided to write a story. She called Casey, who wasn't sure if he even wanted to talk to a reporter. So he prayed about it. "I didn't know what they would do with it," he worried. "I thought maybe they'd write something negative."

But after praying about it, he decided to do what he always does: He just told the truth. He said that if the newspaper wanted to do something negative with it, that was on them. So he spoke with Heslam and told her that he believed the town wasn't within its rights to reject the public rosary. He told her everything that happened, including his friend Rita writing the letter and every detail he could think of. It's easy to remember details when you believe every word you're saying. He even posed for a picture with his rosary.

And to everyone's surprise, that picture ran on the front page of the next edition of *The Boston Herald* with the caption "Let us Pray." Mike didn't know he was on the front page until his phone started ringing and friends began texting. And then the local radio stations began calling.

What did Mike do? He went to work. On his way in, he had to pull over to talk to one radio host who called him. All day at work, the requests started coming in from radio stations and then big television stations like Fox, CNN, and CBS. And lawyers even started calling with offers to represent him. "The calls kept coming in and coming in," he said. "It was getting bigger and bigger."

Mike was unsure what to do. So he did what he always does when he doesn't know what to do. He prayed about it. "I told Jesus if you want this to keep going, I will keep it going," he said. "But if what you needed to be done is done, I won't." He wanted to be sure he wasn't just doing it out of pride. "Sometimes people turn something true, honest, and good into something rotten and bad because of their pride."

His prayer for humility was interrupted by a phone call from a lawyer who told him that the town had just told him they changed their mind and that next year he could hold the rosary on public property. Mike saw that phone call from the lawyer as Jesus's answer to him. (I couldn't help but wonder if this was the first time Jesus had acted through legal counsel.) And then the reporter from the *Herald* also called to say the town would be reversing its decision.

It was the Lord at work, said Mike. "I never lifted a phone. I never called anyone," he said. "This was the Lord's work, and justice was done."

So what did Mike do about all the media requests? Mike had dinner with his son who was heading overseas with the Navy. "We had plans to go out to dinner," he said. "So I didn't call anyone [about the story right away]."

Mike and I talked a lot about faith and prayer. He said he'd be praying to the Virgin Mary and Fr. Vincent Capodanno (The Grunt

Padre) for his son's safety overseas. We talked about the power of prayer, and he told me about his son, and we laughed about my nine-year-old daughter, who'd recently seen a mouse run right by her in church, and so dropped her rosary as she was leading a decade of the rosary in front of hundreds of people.

In the end, I told him I'd pray for him, and especially his son. Mike thanked me. Because he knows that prayers can be very effective.

Discussion Questions

1. Are you comfortable praying out loud in a public setting, or even just at the dinner table with your family? What are some ways you can grow in this area of your spiritual life?

2. Mike's story is a reminder of the influence individual believers can wield in the public square, especially at a local level. When was the last time you wrote an editorial to your local paper, or attended a town meeting? Why is this important?

3. Have you ever participated in a national prayer campaign or some other national Catholic event? Why is it important to take your faith into the public square?

CHAPTER ELEVEN

Fighting the Deadly Silence
Jill Stanek

For it was you who formed my inward parts;
you knit me together in my mother's womb.
I praise you, for I am fearfully and wonderfully made.
Wonderful are your works;
that I know very well.

My frame was not hidden from you,
when I was being made in secret,
intricately woven in the depths of the earth.
Your eyes beheld my unformed substance.

—Psalm 139:13–16

J ill Stanek is now celebrated as one of the foremost defenders of the unborn in the country today. Just a decade ago, she lived much more quietly as a wife, a mother, and a nurse. She didn't know that her life was about to change when she went to work one day. She didn't realize she would be called to stand up for her faith and her belief in the sanctity of life.

It all started when Jill noticed a nursing coworker walking quickly down the hospital hallway with a severely premature baby diagnosed with Down syndrome in her arms. The nurse disappeared into the Soiled Utility Room at the end of the hallway and walked out of the room empty-handed.

As she entered the room and saw the tiny, blanket-wrapped infant gasping for breath, Jill knew she had to stay nearby. "I could not bear the thought of this suffering child dying alone," said Jill. She picked the baby up lovingly and cradled him in her arms.

He weighed just eight ounces, and was just ten inches long—and didn't even have a name. Yet she stayed with him to the end: forty-five minutes, the span of his lifetime. It was all his little body could give him. Jill didn't have the heart to sing to the child or console him with words. She rocked him silently, unable to do more. It took all her strength just to stay in that room and hold him. But there's a lot in holding.

As the minutes crawled by, she heard life continue outside that small room in muffled passing conversations, a high-pitched laugh, and shadows darkening the doorway. To Jill, the most important thing in the world was to hold this baby. She knew that there was no hope for this child. His life would end in this lonely room at the end of a hospital hallway. This tiny, ten-fingered miracle would know no other home than her arms.

Toward the end, the baby's struggle was so quiet that Jill couldn't tell if the baby's soul had whispered out to heaven. She held him up to the light so she could see through his chest wall to see whether his heart was still beating. It wasn't.

After the child was officially pronounced dead, Jill gently folded his tiny arms across his chest, wrapped him tenderly in a shroud, and walked him to the hospital morgue. And as she walked, Jill knew that those forty-five minutes had changed her life forever.

• • •

Some moments of life are like lightning: fast and bright and illuminating. Other life-changing events are more like thunder, sending out a rumble of warning before they roll over us, delayed but inevitable.

Jill had been working at Christ Hospital in Oak Lawn, Illinois, for six years and had worked for a year in the Labor and Delivery Department. Initially she'd taken the position on a part-time basis, working the night shift to accommodate her children's schedules. Yet this life-changing encounter had taken her completely by surprise.

A late bloomer, she didn't receive her college degree until her mid-thirties. She was a mother, a nurse, a wife, a churchgoer. She was happy in the way Americans can be when paychecks arrive weekly, the children are polite, and the roof isn't leaking.

A mother herself, she loved watching the daily miracle of babies being born. At the beginning of each shift, the nurses would gather for a few moments to hand off their assignments to the next shift. One night in 1999, the supervising nurse matter-of-factly said one of the patients on the floor was aborting a second trimester baby diagnosed with Down syndrome. "I was completely shocked," said Jill. She hadn't known Christ Hospital performed abortions.

Everyone else in the room acted as if it were nothing odd at all. Jill remained silent. It wasn't her patient. It had nothing to do with her, she convinced herself. "I went to church on Sunday but I had tons of other things to do," said Jill, "and I really didn't want to associate myself with the crazies in the pro-life movement."

She had a job as a nurse—a good job that she loved. It wasn't up to her to change the world. What could she do anyway, she asked herself. What good would speaking up do? Fearful of the singe of critical glances and whispered comments, she kept her thoughts to herself.

She thought it was the smart thing to do. She needed her job. She and her husband made enough to keep the kids fed and clothed, and they could put a little away for college. She couldn't afford a crusade. She couldn't afford to lose her job. And yet, the very thought of abortions being done in a hospital named after Christ rattled her.

She learned that the method of abortion at Christ Hospital was called "induced labor abortion," now also known as "live birth abortion." In this procedure, doctors do not attempt to kill the baby in the uterus. The goal of the procedure is to deliver a premature baby so that the baby dies either during the delivery or soon afterward.

She wasn't asked to perform the procedure, so she had the option of not dealing with it. Jill could just look the other way and keep her mouth shut. She could just continue working, disturbed and silent...until she encountered that nameless, unwanted infant gasping his life away in that hospital utility room. At that moment, everything changed.

Jill knew she had a choice. She could simply leave and find a new job at a hospital where abortions were not performed, or she could risk everything and work to change Christ Hospital's abortion practice.

Jill questioned herself for days. She prayed. She read the Bible. Finally, an answer came to her in the form of Scripture. She was reading the Bible when some words just jumped up the way Scripture sometimes does, as if the words were written just for her, for that moment.

> If you hold back from rescuing those taken away to death,
> those who go staggering to the slaughter;
> if you say, "Look, we did not know this"—
> does not he who weighs the heart perceive it?
> Does not he who keeps watch over your soul know it?
> And will he not repay all according to their deeds?
> —Proverbs 24:11–12

The decision needed to be made. She badly wanted to quit and just forget about the horror she'd seen. But she felt God was telling her that to quit at that point would be irresponsible and disobedient. "Sure, I might be more comfortable if I left the hospital, but babies would continue to die," she thought.

She spoke to her pastor and with fellow church member Clarke Forsythe, who she knew was involved in the pro-life community. Forsythe was actually a longtime president of Americans United for Life and suggested she send a private letter to the hospital administration.

Clarke helped Jill craft the letter and pointed out the hypocrisy of the hospital's mission statement, which says all people are treated equally under God and asked how that coincided with abortion. "It was a big step for me," said Jill, "but I sent the letter."

For a few days nothing happened. Then a call came that she was to meet with the two chairmen of the obstetrics and gynecology department. They calmly explained to Jill that induced abortion was the "most compassionate" way to abort. They told her it allowed parents to grieve and allowed the baby to be held. They explained this as if allowing a baby to die alone gasping for air was merciful, as if it was the right thing to do when babies were diagnosed with Down syndrome or spina bifida. They talked to Jill as if she was a child unable to understand complexities they bravely faced. They looked at her as if they'd both just realized she was crazy. In the end, they said the procedure wasn't going to stop. It wasn't ever going to stop.

Jill told herself she'd done what could be expected of her. She'd registered her complaint. But the gnawing feeling wouldn't leave her. "I felt I was abandoning the babies if I quit," said Jill.

She sat down with her husband and talked about where she thought God was leading her. "That's the only time my husband got rattled because he knew as well as I did that if I went on with this fight I was facing the possibility of being fired," she said. Jill's income was a substantial part of the family income. They had two teenagers and a little one at home. But one question came to her repeatedly: "How could someone who calls themselves a Christian be more afraid of what other people think than what God thinks?"

The two concluded that they had to do something. Though she knew that many people have fought battles like this behind the scenes to great effect, Jill and her husband decided they weren't going to be sneaky about it. There would be no blurry-faced interviews. No anonymous tips. If Jill was going to fight this she was going to stand up and take this issue head-on.

She took it on because she believed she wouldn't be able to face God if she didn't, not because she had any hope of changing the hospital—never mind the country.

She began carrying her Bible with her every day. She read the stories of those who stood up for God. "Here's the thing, in the Bible, all the apostles were killed. Things didn't end well for most of the people who stood up for Jesus," said Jill. "I knew that chances were I wouldn't be vindicated. I knew that. But I wasn't looking for gratification."

She urged her friends and colleagues to all write letters. Her pastor and Clarke Forsythe encouraged others to write letters, including Cardinal Francis George and former US Surgeon General C. Everett Koop, who wrote a letter to the hospital accusing them of "eugenics."

But nothing happened. Private correspondence wasn't getting it done. She needed to take it one step further. She needed to go public. Once she did that, there was no going back. "I was so scared," she said. "I'm not Joan of Arc."

But she knew it was time to involve others.

• • •

She went on a radio show hosted by Sandy Rios, a popular Chicago talk radio host. For the first time, Jill spoke out publicly about what was occurring at Christ Hospital. And nothing would ever be the same for the part-time night nurse from Illinois.

"It snowballed," said Jill. "I think two factors made it so awful. Nobody had ever heard about this procedure. The other is that it's Christ Hospital. It was so blasphemous."

In July 1999, the issue began getting more press. While still working for the hospital, Jill was handling calls from newspapers and television shows at home.

It soon became apparent from news reports that this practice was not occurring just at Christ Hospital but all over the country. Due to the increasing media scrutiny in 1999, the Illinois attorney general's office investigated the hospital but concluded that the hospital violated no state laws.

The message was getting out. But the overwhelming crush of press was interfering with her relationships at work. Work became difficult. Each weekend, protesters marched outside, even in cold rain, singing hymns and praying under the shadow of the cross atop the hospital. With each new media appearance, the numbers of protestors swelled.

The protests and accusations outside were affecting those inside the hospital. "Everyone was divided," remembers Jill. "The pro-choicers were mad at me. The pro-lifers were mad because that this was going on for twenty years and they didn't know it." Some people just believed Jill was lying and was simply trying to become famous.

Jill was ostracized by many of the women and men she'd considered friends at Christ Hospital. She remembers not being shown family pictures at work when everyone would gather. She was never invited to weddings anymore. Conversations would die a quick death upon her entrance. Looks were exchanged.

In February 2000, Jill was forced to appear before a hospital board of review, where it was alleged that she had "contributed to a negative working environment because of her pro-life activism." However, the hospital's policy did not limit her right to free speech. She won that round, but the hospital was far from done. Jill says she kept her Bible close to her at all times. Passages would jump out at her to aid her. "I know your works. Look, I have set before you an open door, which no one is able to shut. I know that you have but little power, and yet you have kept my word and not denied my name" (Revelation 3:8). When times were roughest, even words from songs on the radio seemed applicable. "I felt constantly being talked to by God," she says. "It was amazing because God is pretty quiet most of the time."

But work became even more unbearable when a letter was posted on the locker-room wall calling Jill a liar. She'd heard that the administration had begun an investigation against her. "They could fire me for anything," she thought. But she made up her mind that she wouldn't get fired over non-professionalism. She worked harder than she'd ever worked before, but the stress was getting to her.

She remembers a few nights sitting with mothers in labor in the darkness, and she could feel a spiritual battle around her. She hated going to work each night, and she prayed, "God you have to help me. I can't do this alone."

That's when Alison Baker came to work on the floor. Jill began talking to her. Alison's brother was a youth minister at Jill's church. The two women had a lot in common. Their friendship made Jill's time on the floor a little easier.

Baker remembers a time when a couple had requested a therapeutic abortion for their twenty-week fetus with spina bifida. The patient delivered her fetus, and the baby was taken to the Soiled Utility Room. During the time the fetus was alive, the patient kept asking Alison when the fetus would die. For an hour and forty-five minutes the baby struggled to live and maintained a heartbeat. The parents grew frustrated. They were obviously not prepared for this long period of time. Alison held the fetus in her arms until the baby finally expired.

The hospital responded to the media exposure with a purely cosmetic change. They opened what they called a Comfort Room, complete with baptismal supplies, gowns, certificates, foot printing equipment, baby bracelets for mementos, a rocking chair, a First Foto machine if parents wanted professional pictures of their aborted baby.

As the issue reached a fever pitch, Jill received a call from out of the blue from someone in Washington, DC, asking her to testify before Congress concerning the Born-Alive Infants Protection Act. The bill declared that any baby born alive and separated from his or her mother, whether through abortion or not, has unalienable rights just as any other American citizen has. This would include the right to medical care—and not just what is termed "comfort care."

They said the bill had been introduced before but only as a theoretical issue in case a baby was born during an abortion. They hadn't known it was common practice. Under the Clinton administration the bill was left to languish. But when George W. Bush entered office, pro-lifers knew they had a friend in the White House.

They said her testimony would be key to finally getting it passed. But on one condition. They also asked if she could find someone else to testify along with her because otherwise she could be too easily dismissed as lying. She needed corroboration.

She asked many nurses on the floor, but they all rejected the idea. They had too much to lose, they said. She felt desperate and sad that even some who believed abortion to be wrong couldn't find the courage to stand up. Jill called upon her friend Alison, who agreed and added that she'd kept a journal of the events at the hospital.

Jill Stanek, the nurse from Illinois, stood up and recounted the desperate breaths of the babies she'd held. She told Congress, "It is not uncommon for a live aborted baby to linger for an hour or two or even longer. At Christ Hospital one of these babies lived for almost an entire eight-hour shift. Some of the babies aborted are healthy, because Christ Hospital will also abort for the life or 'health' of the mother, and also for rape or incest."

Jill was told the bill would likely pass within weeks. She returned to work after testifying, and things only got worse. On August 31, 2001, Jill showed up to work at 11:00 PM. Her boss approached her and said they needed to talk. Jill walked behind her. After all the fear and anguish she'd felt for years over losing her job, it was clear that she was being fired. When she walked into the Human Resources Office, she saw that the head of HR was there.

She knew for sure what was going on then. And her thoughts surprised her. "Oh, thank God," she said. They told her quickly and calmly that she was fired and escorted her out of the hospital. As she was being walked out of the hospital she felt...relieved. "I knew I'd done what I was supposed to do," she said. "I did it." Hospital spokesman Michael Maggio said in reference to her firing, "She was the main reason our hospital became the center of attention in the abortion debate. But that had nothing to do with it."

Meanwhile, the Born-Alive Infants Protection Act, first introduced in July 2000 and passed by the House two months later on a lopsided vote of 380–15 was killed intentionally and anonymously in the Senate by a technicality. It was later, attached as a rider to the Patients' Bill of Rights, but it died again with that legislation.

Jill had lost her job, and the legislation died. But a funny thing happened. Getting fired brought Jill even more notoriety. And after a two-and-a-half-year battle with the hospital, she was free now to openly discuss the horrors of abortion after having seen it with her own eyes. Speaking engagements began coming in from all over the country that made up for her lost income. "It was so nice of God to do that," she says. "I'd been prepared to be a happy martyr."

Soon the bill was once again reintroduced by Senator Rick Santorum. Jill once again went before Congress to testify. She relayed a story about a woman who had chosen to abort her second-trimester baby, having been told that the boy had gross internal and external fetal anomalies. "When her baby was aborted alive, however, he looked fine. The mother became hysterical and screamed for someone to help her baby. A neonatologist was called over, but told the family that the baby had been born too early to help. The mother was so traumatized that she had to be tranquilized, and it was left to the grandparents to hold the little baby boy the half hour that he lived," said Jill.

Following her testimony, everyone in the room fell silent for a moment. The House passed the bill by voice vote, and the Senate agreed to the bill by unanimous consent on July 18, 2002.

On the day President George W. Bush signed the bill into law in 2002, he thanked Jill for her efforts. He said, "It's important that you're here, to send a signal that you're dedicated to the protection of human life. The issue of abortion divides Americans, no question about it. Yet today we stand on common ground. The Born Alive Infants Protection Act establishes a principle.... There is no right to destroy a child who has been born alive. A child who is born has intrinsic worth and must have the full protection of our laws."

The act was important because it was the first federal law passed to limit abortion in any way. Since *Roe* v. *Wade*, all restrictions on abortion had been slipping away with each new ruling by the Supreme Court. Furthermore, Congress rarely involves itself in this critical issue because it is a political landmine.

The *Chicago Sun-Times* called the measure "historic." Dr. Hadley Arkes, the Amherst college professor who wrote the text of the bill for the House Judiciary's Constitution subcommittee said, "It would confirm that Congress can lay hands on this subject [abortion], that Congress may legislate to establish the limits to the right of abortion and even bar certain kinds of abortion."

The passing of the bill was a miracle. A miracle conceived by God and carried through with his help and the perseverance of a part-time night nurse from Illinois who set out to change a hospital and changed the country. "The magnitude of all this is beyond me," she says. "I'm convinced that I'm just a troubled person with stubborn streak and a problem with authority. But he used my faults for good."

When the bill passed, Jill felt like her fight was done. The passage of the federal Born-Alive Infants Protection Act in 2002 has apparently not deterred all doctors from leaving live aborted babies to die without medical intervention. That is why Jill continues the fight as a columnist and as one of the most outspoken defenders of life in the country. She is intent on opening the eyes of American justice. And she is convinced she's not acting alone.

DISCUSSION QUESTIONS

1. Jill Stanek felt very alone and ostracized at work until a new friend stood up for her. Has something like that ever happened in your life?

2. Faith in the sacredness of life drove Jill on despite many obstacles. What are some of the ways you have seen others uphold the sacred nature of life?

3. This story speaks of "lightning bolt" revelations and "thundering" insights that build up gradually over time. Can you think of instances in your own life when you experienced these things? Which tend to have the most lasting effect, and why?

CHAPTER TWELVE

Victim 0001

Father Mychal Judge

Whoever does not take up the cross and follow me is not worthy of me. Those who find their life will lose it, and those who lose their life for my sake will find it.

—Matthew 10:39

You do what God has called you to do. You get on that rig, you go out and do the job. No matter how big the call, no matter how small, you have no idea of what God is calling you to do, but God needs you. He needs me. He needs all of us. God needs us to keep supporting each other, to be kind to each other, to love each other.

Father Mychal Judge, OFM

Mass for Firefighters

September 10, 2001

J ust one day after he preached these words at his last homily, Fr. Mychal would rush out of his rectory upon hearing that the World Trade Center had been hit by two planes in a terrorist attack. Bodies already lay in the streets around the buildings. Fr. Mychal was met by New York City Mayor Rudolph Giuliani, who asked him to pray for the city in its most tragic hour. The mayor also reportedly urged Fr. Mychal to stay with him, but the priest insisted he needed to be with his men.

As the chaplain of the New York City firefighters, Fr. Mychal prayed over many of those who had fallen or leapt from the tower, and he entered the lobby of the World Trade Center North Tower to offer aid and prayers for the rescuers.

New York Daily News columnist Michael Daly reported that Judge, bent over victims, repeatedly prayed aloud, "Jesus, please end this right now! God, please end this!"

At 9:59 AM, the South Tower collapsed. Heavy debris exploded into the North Tower lobby, killing many inside. Fr. Mychal was one of the casualties.

A policeman, two firemen, an FDNY emergency medical technician, and one civilian volunteer found and carried Fr. Mychal's body out of the North Tower. That moment was captured by a Reuters photographer, Shannon Stapleton, and became perhaps the most iconic image of the tragedy.

Fr. Mychal's body was laid before the altar of St. Peter's Catholic Church before being taken to the medical examiner. He is officially labeled by NYC as victim 0001 of the World Trade Center attack. Fr. Mychal Judge's name is on Panel S-18 of the National September 11 Memorial's South Pool.

At the official body identification, it was former NYPD officer Steven McDonald who reportedly identified Fr. Mychal's body. A former US Navy hospital corpsman and third-generation police officer, McDonald met Fr. Mychal after being shot three times by a fifteen-year-old boy, which left him paralyzed from the neck down and in need of a ventilator.

McDonald says he was bitter and angry over the shooting. He credits Fr. Mychal with reaffirming his faith in God. "He, more than anything…reaffirmed, reaffirmed my faith in God, and [said] that it was important to me to forgive the boy who shot me," he told a *Democracy Now* reporter. "And I'm alive today because of that." McDonald reached out to the young man who had shot him and had been sent to jail. They spoke on the phone and they became friends, according to McDonald.

• • •

Fr. Mychal worked with the homeless, AIDS victims, and anyone who needed to be reminded of Christ's love. Born in Brooklyn, New York, in 1933, Robert Emmett Judge was one of a pair of twins. His sister Dympna was born two days later, and they were both baptized in St. Paul's Church.

It wasn't an easy life. The Great Depression was hard on everyone. Judge's father died when he was only six, and he was forced to earn income for the family shining shoes at Penn Station. When he could, he would often walk across the street to St. Francis of Assisi Church, where he was always impressed by the friars there.

"God gave me the vocation, considering my person, to be a follower of St. Francis, where I truly believe I fit in perfectly," he was quoted as saying in *Father Mychal Judge: An Authentic American Hero.* "I've never wanted to be anything else."

Educated at Catholic schools, he entered the seminary at age fifteen. Upon graduation, he enrolled at St. Bonaventure University. Upon receiving his religious habit, he received the name Fallon Michael, which he later shortened and changed to Mychal (which is the Gaelic spelling.) He professed his vows as a full member of the Franciscan Order in 1958. After completing his theological studies at Holy Name College Seminary in Washington, DC, he was ordained a priest in 1961.

After serving in parishes in Boston, New Jersey, and the Bronx, he served as assistant to the president of Siena College. Fr. Mychal battled alcoholism, but with the support of Alcoholics Anonymous, he became sober in 1978. In 1986, Fr. Mychal returned home, in a way, as he was assigned to St. Francis of Assisi Church in Manhattan, the church he had sat in as a young boy.

In 1992, Fr. Mychal was appointed chaplain to the New York City fire department. But Fr. Mychal was already famous in the city for ministering to the hungry and homeless, the drug addicts and alcoholics, those sick with HIV and AIDS, the grieving, gays and lesbians, and anyone who needed help. In fact, Fr. Mychal considered himself homosexual, yet remained celibate as a priest.

Fr. Mychal saw the city as his ministry. His simple prayer, according to Beliefnet.com, was, "Lord, take me where you want me to go, let me meet who you want me to meet, tell me what you want me to say, and keep me out of your way."

God took Fr. Mychal many places, even to the top of a ladder, pleading with a gunman to spare his wife and baby. Fr. Michael Duffy, OFM, recalled in his eulogy a time when he returned to the friary only to be told, "There's a hostage situation in Carlstadt and Mychal Judge is up there."

> I got in the car and drove there: A man on the second floor with a gun pointed to his wife's head and the baby in her arms. He threatened to kill her. There were several people around, lights, policemen and a fire truck. And where was Mychal Judge? Up on the ladder in his habit, on the top of the ladder, talking to the man through the window of the second floor. I nearly died because in one hand he had his habit out like this, because he didn't want to trip.
>
> So, he was hanging on the ladder with one hand. He wasn't very dexterous, anyway. His head was bobbing like, "Well, you know, John, maybe we can work this out. This really isn't the way to do it. Why don't you come downstairs, and we'll have a cup of coffee and talk this thing over?"
>
> I thought, "He's going to fall off the ladder. There's going to be gunplay." Not one ounce of fear did he show. He was

telling him, "You know, you're a good man, John. You don't need to do this." I don't know what happened, but he put the gun down and the wife and the baby's lives were saved.

Fr. Mychal simply wished to go where God needed him. And he could never refuse God anything. "The wonderful thing is saying yes and accepting God's grace. We could say no and walk away. But when we say yes and go forward, great and wonderful things will happen," Fr. Mychal reportedly said. "It takes courage in the midst of fear, but you do it with the grace of God."

Great courage is what Fr. Mychal showed the world throughout his life and on the day when the world needed courage. On the darkest day, when the world needed to be reminded of Christ's love, Fr. Mychal Judge showed us that light.

DISCUSSION QUESTIONS

1. Fr. Mychal gave all for others. His courage has inspired millions. Did you learn anything new about him from reading this, about how his faith informed his life?

2. Fr. Mychal reached out to the dispossessed. What opportunities have you found in your local parish or community where you might be able to make a difference?

3. "The wonderful thing is saying yes and accepting God's grace." Can you name a time when you did this?

CHAPTER THIRTEEN

Losing Fear

Heather Mercer

While he was still speaking, someone came from the leader's house to say, "Your daughter is dead; do not trouble the teacher any longer." When Jesus heard this, he replied, "Do not fear. Only believe, and she will be saved."

—Luke 8:49-50

Letting go of fear can be one of the most difficult things a Christian can do. Heather Mercer had every reason to fear as she was taken prisoner by the Taliban and made a pawn after the tragic events of September 11. Her journey to acceptance played out on the world stage and has served to inspire so many.

Heather thought it peculiar that none of the children who usually mobbed around her weren't there when she went outside. Other than the car waiting for her, she was alone on the Afghanistan street. There were no beggars. A surge of fear rose in her, but she did her best to ignore it. She was fearful because she had shown *The Jesus Film* to a Muslim family, and it was still in her briefcase. She was fearful because she was a Christian missionary in a place where being a Christian was illegal. But she didn't see anything except the car waiting to take her to meet her fellow missionaries, including her friend Dayna Curry. When Heather climbed in, her driver, whom she knew well, looked nervously at her in the rear-view. Their eyes connected for a moment.

Heather knew something was wrong but wasn't sure what it was. After her driver traveled just a short distance, he inexplicably slowed down and then stopped for a strange man who jumped into the front seat of the car. And the driver accelerated with the silent man in the seat next to him.

With fear rising into panic, she asked her driver what was going on, but neither the man nor the driver responded. They simply stared straight ahead, ignoring her. After traveling a short distance more, another man jumped into the car, this time in the back-seat right next to Heather. Attempting to appear calm, she simply opened her door and attempted to flee the car, but the man's hand shot out, grabbing her. She quickly looked around and noticed she was at a Taliban checkpoint, surrounded by armed guards.

There was nowhere to go.

She sat back down into the car resignedly, holding her briefcase tightly to her. When the car pulled up to a nondescript government building, she spotted Dayna, her friend and colleague for Shelter Now International, in the backseat of a car. Clearly, she was a prisoner as well. The guards dragged Heather over to the other car where Dayna was sitting and ripped the briefcase from her hands. Heather looked at Dayna, and though she was scared of what was happening and what might happen, she said to her friend through the window, "It's OK. God is with us."

That faith would be tested over the next four months while she remained a prisoner of the Taliban, especially after the events on September 11 occurred and American forces geared up for war.

• • •

As a child, Heather had never done the expected thing. She grew up as a middle-class American, the product of divorce. She was rebellious and athletic. Although a nominal Christian, she had never really considered faith an important part of her life. It was a Christian friend who inspired Heather to reconsider the importance of faith in her life by inviting her to a Christian concert. There, Heather was shocked to hear a message of Christ which was relevant to her everyday life. This was not a Christ of rules and dogma, these were promises from an alive and risen Savior. Bowled over and in tears, she vowed to follow Jesus that day. And she did it the way she did everything—with all she had. She chose to attend the Christian college Baylor University, where she worked in campus ministry.

One day while reading the Bible, a passage caught her attention which said, "He defended the cause of the poor and needy.... 'Is this not what it means to know me?' declares the Lord." That intimate connection between faith and service deeply impressed the young girl. Her life would never be the same. Soon, the thought of going overseas to serve the poor and oppressed became a desire which turned into a need.

She prayed, not for her own happiness, but for God to send her to the hardest place possible to serve Christ. She pleaded with the Lord to be sent where others would not go.

And that was when her church announced a need for missionaries to go to Afghanistan in the summer of 1998. In a rush of excitement, she signed up to spend her summer vacation in one of the most dangerous places on earth for a Christian.

Her trip did not go as expected.

On the day she arrived in Afghanistan, the Taliban declared that all foreign aid workers must locate themselves in a bombed-out building with no electricity or water. That day, while she was being given a tour of a medical facility, her guide warned her that armed Taliban were in the clinic and had just kidnapped an employee. She was told to run, to hide in a house. She did. And then it was a race to get Heather and her fellow student missionaries out of the country before the Taliban manned all the border crossings. She escaped, but even as she boarded a plane in Pakistan to return home, she knew in her heart that she would one day return.

Heather felt called by God to return to the Middle East as a missionary.

She returned to Afghanistan the following summer, staying in the home of fellow missionaries. She grew to love the people and truly believed that was where God wanted her to serve.

After graduating from Baylor, she signed on to to be a missionary for a three-year term starting in March 2001. Her mother begged her not to go, warning her that there was now a death penalty in Afghanistan for anyone who converted from Islam to any other religion. Her mother said she feared that if Heather went, she'd never see her again.

Heather Mercer and Dayna Curry worked together in Afghanistan, working with anyone who needed help, including families of the Taliban who needed it. Shelter Now International was responsible for building houses, repairing or rebuilding wells, and creating medical clinics. When asked why they were doing what they were doing, they would share their stories about how Jesus changed them. This, in a country, where it was illegal to evangelize.

The home they lived in had previously been an artillery ware-house for mercenaries with a bunker for a backyard. Packs of hungry dogs gathered around the garbage piled in front of their house, making going outdoors at night difficult if not dangerous. But they made the home as hospitable as possible and would often have neighborhood women over for tea or take them shopping for food or necessities.

The two women loved what they were doing. The Taliban, however, were a fearful presence driving through the streets with angry and distrustful looks, their arms resting on their guns.

Heather said they often had hatred in their eyes for the missionaries. One armed Taliban soldier spat on Heather. Another time she was grabbed at night by an armed Taliban agent, and only because of Dayna's screams did the man let go.

Danger for the missionaries were everywhere. But the two persisted in helping anyone they could help, including the families of Taliban guards.

While Heather was taking a language course so she could better converse with Afghanis, she also found time to visit the ill in a local medical clinic. One day she said a prayer to Jesus out loud for the mother of a friend who was ill there. Soon, others in the clinic, some seriously ill, were asking this strange blonde woman to pray to Jesus for them as well. It was around that time that she saw a woman with terrible burns all over her body who had set herself on fire after being forced to marry a Taliban guard. She wasn't alone. Others had done the same to escape the oppressive poverty and abuse.

Moved, Heather asked the clinic if she could help even though she had very limited medical skills and didn't know the language all that well. She still remembers one girl, a fourteen-year-old with cerebral palsy, named Lida. She remembers finding her covered in her own fecal matter with flies buzzing all around her. Heather would often clean her up and get her to use her walker for brief stretches. As Lida couldn't speak, Heather's inability to speak the language hardly mattered. She would feed and clean the young girl with a smile. When the young girl was happy, she would clap. That was how the two would communicate. Heather would pray for Lida. Sometimes she would sing. Lida would clap.

Heather was arranging for Lida to be adopted by a family when she was arrested. She never saw Lida again, though she thinks of her often and prays that she found someone to love her and care for her.

On the night of August 3, Heather and Dayna played *The Jesus Film* on a CD on the computer for a family that had shown great interest in getting to know Jesus. After the film, Heather warned the family that it was dangerous for them to follow Jesus. "It is dangerous for me as well," she said. "But it is more dangerous for you."

And then she stepped outside and got into the car. And her life changed.

The two missionaries were sent to a prison for women that was insufferably hot. That first night and for many nights after, they would lay a sheet outside in the courtyard to lie on. That first night they prayed for strength. And they sang songs of praise. Other inmates called out to them from their window, asking them to continue. Though they didn't know the words, they too were comforted by their songs of praise.

The following day, the relentless interrogations started. The first round lasted three days in a small room. The interrogators angrily insisted they sign documents in another language, but the two, fearing that they were being framed, refused. Eventually, they agreed only to sign their own answers to questions in English so that their words could not be twisted. They soon learned that their arrest was part of a larger plan as many other missionaries were arrested in the days that followed.

Their interrogations soon focused squarely on *The Jesus Film*. The Taliban had found it. Heather and Dayna tried not to lie, but at times they simply refused to answer a question about it for fear that others would be detained or worse. Interrogators grew frustrated, and a punishment of death became a very real possibility for the two women. In fact, they heard in media reports that the death penalty was indeed being considered for them. Heather didn't immediately pray to be delivered from the Taliban but instead prayed for the strength to face death for Christ. She feared that she wasn't strong enough and prayed that God would supply her that strength.

Over the months that followed, the situation in the prison became deplorable. Heather recalls the ever-present rodents, her head becoming infested with lice, and parasitic worms ten inches long invading her body, which she discovered only when she coughed one up and pulled it out of her mouth. It was still alive.

In late August and early September of 2001, Heather and Dayna's plight dominated the news. Their parents were interviewed on the network morning shows and evening newscasts. On September 8, Heather and Dayna were moved to another prison. As they stepped out of the van, they saw a throng of media standing at the gate of the courthouse taking video and shooting pictures of them.

The following day, they appeared in front of the court of eighteen judges—the Supreme Court of Afghanistan. The lead judge asked where their lawyer was. Panic set in. They'd had little contact with anyone outside the prison, certainly not a lawyer. They didn't even know what the charges were. Heather asked the judge how they could obtain a lawyer, but the judge's answer in response was vague. They were returned to their jail shortly after, still unsure how they could obtain a lawyer or how to proceed at all.

The young women were allowed some brief visits with their parents, who had traveled to Afghanistan just to see them. It was after one such visit that a guard told the two young women that two planes had crashed into each other over New York City and that hundreds were dead. The guard said that America believed Afghanistan may have had something to do with it.

It was September 11.

The following evening there were bombs exploding around the city, clearly fighting between the Taliban and the Northern Alliance. Heather panicked. She knew her parents were still in the city near the prison and begged to hear from them. The guards, tired of having a crying woman on their hands, had notes passed from her parents to her and finally allowed a phone call.

In a conversation with her father, Heather said that she'd heard what happened in America. Her father seemed surprised that she'd heard. He added that the situation would likely make things harder for her. He then said that he, along with all Westerners, were being evacuated because of what happened on September 11.

It was then she knew that something much worse than an airplane crash had occurred. They soon learned the full extent of the horrors of 9/11. She prayed for the families of those affected. She prayed for her country. While she prayed, she understood that her life was in even more danger than it had been before.

In the days that followed, they were moved to yet another location. The missionaries feared that they were now being held captive in a military stronghold to prevent the US from bombing their location. They soon heard bombs dropping in Kabul. The bombs sometimes dropped so devastatingly close that their prison walls shook.

Soon after, a journalist who had been captured by the Taliban, told Dayna and Heather that she'd heard that Mullah Omar was attempting to negotiate with President George W. Bush to promise to not bomb Afghanistan if he promised to return the missionaries. Their lives had become a negotiating tactic. But both knew this would never happen. They both knew that American bombs would soon be landing in Afghanistan, and they weren't sure if the US knew where they were.

One day, a US drone flew over the prison, low enough that a great deal of shooting from anti-aircraft guns exploded from the ground. Heather recalls getting under the bed for protection. That was when she absolutely knew war was coming.

The bombing started. With fear rising, Heather spent much of the time under the bed, praying incessantly for the group's safety. A woman who worked in the prison, who was pregnant with twins, suddenly went into premature labor. The missionaries begged the Taliban guards for help, but they told the woman, "Stop whining and crying. Get back to work."

Even Heather was shocked by what she calls their "utter brutality."

The woman lay on the bed as bombs exploded nearby. As she lay on the bed, Heather reached her hand up from underneath, and they held hands and cried together as the prison walls shook and the night sky turned red. Heather sang "The Lord Is My Shepherd" until her jailer fell asleep from exhaustion.

"There was a real defining sense of God's presence that night," she says. "There was still anxiety, but we knew Jesus was there, too. He hadn't forgotten us. Whatever happened, we would have grace to deal with it."

The bombs would come in at odd times and for no set time periods. The Northern Alliance had no idea where Dayna and Heather were, and even if they did, they had no sophisticated guidance systems for their bombs. So from one moment to the next, a bomb could land anywhere, anytime. Exhausted from the inability to sleep through the bombings, she did an amazing thing. She gave her life over to God. Completely. She let go of her fears and decided that whether she lived or died was up to him. She ceased putting her hope in diplomats, judges, or war. Her trust would be in God completely. She prayed not merely for her own safety but that this war would help Afghanistan in the long run. She prayed for the safety of the people. She prayed for George W. Bush and the American people.

Soon, they heard that the Northern Alliance had the Taliban on the run. They knew this was good news for the country, but they had no idea whether a desperate and retreating Taliban was good for them.

In November, a guard rushed in and told them they had to go.

They were whisked into a van. They noticed that all the lights around the prison were off. They were brought to a basement of a nearby building. The Northern Alliance was close to Kabul, they heard.

At some point in the night, armed guards woke them and insisted that they leave. Now! They were told they were returning to their old prison, but they knew that was a lie. They were led to the back of a truck, where they sat on rocket launchers and weapons. They insisted to know where they were being taken, but the armed guards only mocked them. The missionaries feared this was the end. Heather sang, "There is a light in the darkness and his name is Jesus." She began reading from the Bible out loud to her fellow missionaries. In the book *Prisoners of Hope*, Dayna wrote of Heather that at that moment, "She who had been afraid, now confidently comforted us in our distress."

Jesus had stripped Heather of her fears and her distress. She would do everything she could for Christ and leave the rest up to him.

They believed they were being driven to their death, and they sang worship to Jesus. They were forced to sleep that night in a large shipping container while, once again, the guards mocked them with sneers.

In the morning they were taken to a bombed-out building as American bombs dropped nearby. They hastily gathered themselves for a prayer when shouting and gunfire erupted just outside their makeshift prison. Their Taliban guards ran outside, disappearing down the street. When the gunfire stopped, there was silence. And then someone was banging forcefully on the front door. The sound of heavy footfalls boomed on the floor below and then raced up the stairs to them. As the footfalls approached, Heather was certain it was the Taliban returning to kill them before they could be saved. She said a prayer that she would die worshiping Jesus.

A beardless man holding a rocket launcher bounded into the room and looked up, surprised to see the missionaries there. Then he said something that surprised all of them. He said, "Hello," in English.

And then he told them they were free, as the Taliban had fled.

After some celebrating, they were led to another location that was owned by a Taliban warrior who quickly changed sides when the Northern Alliance gained the upper hand. A pickup spot for a helicopter was arranged. As they raced through the town under cover of night, they dared not speak English for fear that many Taliban were still around. The missionaries arrived at an old airfield and shortly after heard the helicopters circling above them only to retreat time and again into the darkness.

The missionaries believed they couldn't be seen by the pilot. Heather grew desperate, knowing that if they were not saved that night, they could fall back into Taliban hands. In fact, the noise from the helicopter was drawing attention. She saw a light go on in a nearby house. Someone was searching nearby with a flashlight. Suddenly a man appeared behind them, asking them who they were. The armed guard with them told them that the situation was becoming too dangerous and they should leave. The city was waking up around them. The Taliban could find them. Others, interested in ransom, could take them. He insisted they leave.

Heather said she had no intention of leaving that airfield. She thought that the Taliban knew where they were by now, and it was either they get out of the country now or they'd be found. Heather started going through other people's bags looking for matches. She miraculously found some. She ripped off her head scarf and lit it ablaze in order to get the helicopter's attention. A light in the darkness. Quickly, Dayna did the same.

Now, everyone knew where they were. It was now or never. The helicopter dropped down so close that the dirt swirled around the missionaries. They were sure they'd been seen, but it retreated once again into the night sky.

Heather and Dayna saw figures approaching them. They tensed. And out of the swirl of dust, they recognized the figures as American soldiers. They were saved. As she boarded the copter, a soldier told her that his family had been praying for their safe return and that he was honored to be part of their rescue.

Dayna and Heather made it home to their families. Their return was covered extensively by the media, and the two met with President George W. Bush in the Oval Office.

• • •

The courage to withstand the threat of death and to remain solid in her faith until she finally made it home is amazing enough. But even more heroic is that Heather returned to the Middle East.

"God called me to the Muslim world when I was nineteen," she says. "That calling has never changed."

She says she can't help but think, "God didn't save us from that to just tell the same story the rest of our lives."

"I think I felt that I've been given much, and that I have been saved for a purpose. There's still a job to do," she says. "Millions of Muslims haven't heard the Gospel."

Looking back, Heather says, "Part of walking with Jesus involves suffering. Just because there was suffering and persecution doesn't mean something wrong happened. Something right happened. I believe God was using us."

Heather created an organization called Global Hope which focuses on reaching Muslims. She works extensively in Northern Iraq, spending a good deal of each year there. She even married an Iraqi Christian.

She knows better than anyone what she's up against. She has witnessed the brutal slaughter of Christians. She has witnessed the mass exodus of Christians from many parts of Iraq.

"We are in a historic spiritual climate shift," she says. "The powers that be are attempting to rewrite and redraw the map of the Middle East. It is a political shift, a geographic shift, and a spiritual shift."

"We're seeing the largest mass exodus of Christians perhaps in history," she says. "Literally whole cities that a generation ago were 50 percent Christian, like Nineveh and Mosul—today there is not one single Christian left in Mosul."

"Last June, ISIS came in, took over the city and declared all Christians have to convert to Islam, pay a tax, or be executed," she says. "But I believe God hasn't forsaken Mosul."

While she agrees that "it looks grim," she also believes that "at the same time God is awakening Muslims to the reality of what Islam is."

She says many Muslims are converting to Christianity. "God is definitely moving," she says. "The needs are tremendous."

"In this day and time there will be persecution in the name of Christ," she says. "People turn a blind eye. It's too dangerous. It's too scary. But everybody can make a difference. Everyone can do a small thing."

Study Group Questions

1. Does fear limit you in some way? How?
2. Have you ever shared your faith with someone from a different faith tradition? What are some good ways to build bridges with people who do not share your beliefs?
3. What are some ways that you can stand in solidarity with the persecuted Christians in other parts of the world, such as Iraq?

CHAPTER FOURTEEN

The Friend of My Final Moment

The Monks of Tibhirine

Let mutual love continue. Do not neglect to show hospitality to strangers, for by doing that some have entertained angels without knowing it.

—Hebrews 13:1

Our Lady of Atlas was founded in 1934 by monks from the Abbey of Our Lady of Liberation in Tibhirine. In 1830 the French had conquered Algeria to stop pirating in the Mediterranean, and settlements soon followed that lasted for more than a century, until political movements starting in 1938 began to agitate for a sovereign Algerian state. In the wake of World War II, French soldiers were sent to put down the uprising; among them was Christian de Cherge.

In 1959, during the time of his own military service, Christian was stationed in Algeria. At this time, a mutual friendship grew between Christian and Mohamed, a village policeman who worked for the French authorities (a position that put him at risk for violence by the National Liberation Army, as did his friendship with Christian). One evening the two were walking when Christian was accosted by a violent group. Mohamed intervened and rescued his friend from danger, only to be assassinated himself on the following day.

In this act of giving his life, Mohamed dramatized for Christian the implications of his own Gospel: that no greater love exists than in giving one's life for another. From that point on, Christian's own calling would be a supreme devotion to the embodiment of that love, lived out particularly in relation to the Islam that Mohamed had concretely dramatized for him and in Algeria, where he would make his vow of monastic stability.

In his friend, Christian saw Christ. It wasn't that he believed there to be no difference between Christianity and Islam, but Christian believed in a loving God who moved in the hearts of all.

• • •

In October 1993 an armed group of Islamic fanatics known locally as the Groupe Islamique Armé, or the GIA, kidnapped three French consuls and demanded that all foreigners leave the country within a month, by December 1. This was the same day that a little known monk named Dom Christian de Cherge sat down to write a letter to his worried mother. It would later come to be known as his testament and make his name known throughout the world.

Rumors and threats from armed fanatics soon became a bloody reality in the streets of Algeria. The violence focused mainly on the small but active Christian community throughout the country. Thousands were now marching under the bloody banner of Islamic fascism. This violent reality could not be shut out by monastery walls; only a few miles from "Our Lady of Atlas," on December 14, 1993, twelve Christian Croats working at a nearby hydraulic plant in Tamesguida were kidnapped and beheaded. The monks had known the Croats well and mourned and prayed for their friends.

Just ten days later on Christmas Eve at 7:15 PM, the murderous Sayat-Attya came to the darkened gates of the Trappist monastery. This was the same group that had led the slaughter of the

Croatians just weeks before. He called out loudly to speak to the "pope of the place."

Dom Christian de Cherge was no meek monk and came out demanding to know why anyone would attempt to bring arms into a house of peace. Sayat-Attya menacingly told him that a one-month grace period had just expired in which the GIA had warned all foreigners to leave the country. The monks had known of this warning.

Dom Christian, a French Algerian like the other monks, understood that the fate of all the monks could lie in the balance of his answer. He understood that pleading would do little but empower the Muslim fanatics, so he hastily decided to take a different tack.

"This is a house of peace," he proclaimed boldly. "No one has ever come in here carrying weapons. If you want to talk with us, come in, but leave your arms outside. If you cannot do that, we will talk outside."

The armed fanatics were put on their heels slightly as people don't typically admonish armed marauders. The armed men dismissed Christian's demands and made three requests: They declared that the wealth of the monastery be given to the armed men. Further, they demanded that the monastery's doctor leave the monastery and come out into the mountains with them to care for their sick and wounded. Finally, they were to hand over all of their medicine.

Dom Christian told the men that their medicine was available to all who needed it, but only in the monastery. As for the money, the monk replied, they were a monastic community that worked for their bread each day, giving whatever was left to the poor. As for the doctor, Dom Christian explained, Br. Luc was eighty-two years old, and his asthma made it impossible for him to travel. But help was always available at the monastery to those who asked. Sensing that further conversation was useless, Dom Christian then announced that the monks were in the middle of their preparation to celebrate Christ's birth and brought an end to the negotiations.

To the shock of everyone, Emir Sayat-Attya, the leader of the terrorists, apologized: "In that case, please excuse us. We did not know." Then, just before leaving he turned and ominously promised to return.

Dom Christian and the other monks knew that this was no empty threat. That night the monks began a serious discussion, deciding whether or not to leave the increasingly violent country. Some argued reasonably that the Christian presence had been all but wiped out locally during the murderous previous years, and the people were trapped between the various governmental, military, and fundamentalist Islamic factions. Parishes had only a few faithful. On the other hand, the monk's daily acts of charity and love reached far beyond the Christians in the area to many Muslims in desperate need with clothes, medicine, and compassion.

Brother Luke had ministered to the sick in a free clinic at the monastery for five decades. Dom Christian, the prior, was a leader of a Muslim-Christian group called Ribat es Salam (Bond of Peace) that brought religious leaders throughout Algeria to the monastery for dialogue. The guest house was usually full. Local villagers frequently came to the gatehouse for a drink of water, to use the telephone, or to dictate a letter. Sometimes they would bring olives to be pressed at the monastery mill and have the monks store the olive oil and distribute it to them as needed. These monks were a vital part of their community and an example of godliness.

All this was taken into account by the monks, who found it difficult to depart the mountain they'd grown to love. It was a visit from Archbishop Tessier which helped them to reflect more deeply on what it would mean to the other religious communities and Christians in Algeria if the whole monastery were to leave. He left the decision with them, knowing it could be a death sentence to oblige them under obedience to stay.

Meanwhile, the prefect of Medea called Dom Christian, urging the monks to move into the city under the government's protection. Similarly, the Algerian government proposed that police be stationed in an unused building in the monastery for protection.

The monks met on December 31 to decide what to do. They refused both offers of protection, unwilling to give the impression that they were taking sides in the conflict or to allow weapons inside the gates, even for protection. These men were determined to live out the Gospel faithfully in their neighborhood, their country, and their world.

Contrary to what some thought, Dom Christian was not naïve. He understood that his life was in danger and that the decision to stay would likely cost him his life. In response, the prefect sent a letter to the monks, absolving himself of all responsibility for their fate. In the country outside the gates, violence exploded with an estimated one thousand murders a week.

Meanwhile, the monks lived out their daily vows, rising in the middle of the night for vigils and several hours of prayer followed by Mass; work in the morning and afternoon interspersed with brief prayers; meals in common, in silence or with a public reading; and night prayers and a blessing by the abbot before retiring. The monks decided to stay and continued in their resolve to not abandon their community and show a sign of peace and that Christ is still with all of them. But because of the violence, the monks stopped taking novices into the monastery.

Dom Christian believed he had a life to give, just as his friend Mohamed had sacrificed his life for him so many years ago. Dom Christian was intent upon staying at the monastery, intent to prove to all sides that peace was possible.

The violence around the monastery increased. The Muslim fanatics struck at Christians in particular with brutality. First, a

Little Sister of the Assumption, Paule Hélène Saint Raymond, and
a Marist brother, Henri Vergès, were killed by Islamic militants on
May 8, 1994. It was Vergès's death which caused Dom Christian
to reflect:

> His death seems so natural, so fitting to a long life entirely
> given, intentionally, from the first. He seems to me to belong
> to the category of those whom I call "martyrs of hope,"
> who are never spoken of because it is in the patience of daily
> life that they spill all their blood. I understand "monastic
> martyrdom" in the same way. And it is this instinct that
> currently leads us not to change anything, unless toward a
> permanent effort of conversion (but even in this there is no
> change!).

Two Augustinians, Caridad María Alvarez and Esther Alonso,
were killed in October 1994 as they left a church in Algiers. In a
letter to the abbot general, Dom Christian described the funeral for
the two women, which deeply affected the small remnant of what
had once been a large church in Algiers:

> The celebration had a beautiful climate of serenity and self-
> offering. It brought together a tiny church whose still living
> members all realize that the logic of their presence must
> now include the possibility of violent death. For many, it
> is an occasion for a new and radical immersion in the very
> charism of their congregation...as well as a return to the
> very fount of their first calling. Furthermore, it is clear that
> all desire that none of these Algerians, to whom our conse-
> cration links us in the name of the love that God has for
> them, should wound that love by killing any of us, any of
> our Brothers.

The killing of Christians continued. Two more nuns, Odile Prévost
and a Sr. Chantal, both members of Charles Foucauld's Little Sisters
of the Sacred Heart, were killed. Then Jean Chevillar, Christian

Cheissel, Alain Dieulangard, and Charles Deckers—four White Fathers, a community with longstanding ties to Africa, were killed in Tizi Ouzou. When asked by friends in France how things were going, Brother Paul wrote back with dark humor, "My head is still on my shoulders."

An entry in the journal of Brother Christopher, dated February 19, 1996, shows that the monks knew what awaited them: "Violence and bloodshed in the country again and again," he writes, and then he asks Christ, "When will the time come to be planted at Tibhirine: planted in you, my Beloved?"

And this entry on March 19, 1996, the Feast of St. Joseph: "Today is the anniversary of my consecration to Mary," he writes, recalling his final profession. "Yes, I continue to choose you, Mary, with Joseph, in the communion of all the saints.... Like the beloved disciple, I take you into my home. Near you, I am what I should be: offered."

Another armed group arrived at the Trappist community, claiming to want to use the monastery telephone and promising the monks that they would not be harmed. The monks refused to let them enter, and the group left back into the mountain. Dom Christian and his colleagues knew that the threats would only increase. When some sisters of Our Lady of the Apostles also fell to armed bands and were murdered, a visiting papal delegate at the funeral told the Trappists that he admired their decision (to remain in the monastery because of their commitment to the people) but encouraged them not to ignore basic prudence and discretion.

Father Christopher Lebreton, another of the Trappists, wrote of how the slow, stressful process affected them all.

> There is something unique in our way of being Church: how we react to events, how we wait for them and live them out in practice. It has to do with a certain awareness, that we are responsible not for doing something, but for being

something here, in response to Truth and to Love. Are we facing eternity? There is a sense of that. "Our Lady of Atlas, a sign on the mountains," *signum in montibus*, as our coat of arms declares.... The martyr no longer desires anything for himself, not even the glory of martyrdom.

Dom Christian in particular, with his long experience of Algiers and of life, reflects in a document that has become known as his testament:

I have lived long enough to know that I am an accomplice in the evil which seems, alas, to prevail in the world, even in the evil which might blindly strike me down. I would like, when the time comes, to have a moment of spiritual clarity which would allow me to beg forgiveness of God and of my fellow human beings, and at the same time forgive with all my heart the one who will strike me down. I could not desire such a death. It seems to me important to state this. I do not see, in fact, how I could rejoice if the people I love were indiscriminately accused of my murder. It would be too high a price to pay for what will perhaps be called the "grace of martyrdom."

During the night of March 27, 1996, seven of the monks were abducted in a two-month ordeal that would stretch out almost until Pentecost. A month after the abduction, a GIA communiqué offered several reasons why the monks were seized and several conditions for their safe release. Among the reasons given for why the action was licit, the GIA emir, Abou Abdel Rahmân Amîn (popularly called Djamel Zitouni), argued that the previous protection (aman) was improper because the monks "have not ceased to invite Muslims to be evangelized. They have continued to display their Christian slogans and symbols and to commemorate their feasts with solemnity."

In short, the monks were to be killed for helping Muslims.

They'd be killed for being loving Christians. Gone was the mutual religious respect manifested by the dark visitors on Christmas Eve two years earlier.

Over the two years, the country had spiraled into violence and fanaticism. Citing selectively from Muslim law, the emir also stated: "It is therefore licit to apply to these monks what applies to unbelievers who are prisoners of war, namely: death, slavery or exchange for Muslim prisoners." They demanded the release of GIA members held by Algeria and France with this threat: "The choice is yours. If you liberate, we shall liberate. If you do not free your prisoners, we will cut the throats of ours. Glory to God."

Governments who are given ultimatums by terrorists fear that they cannot give in without inviting more terrorism. That reasoning guided the French and Algerian authorities, though they sought ways to negotiate a solution. President Jacques Chirac stated formally on May 20 that there would be no negotiations with the terrorists regarding an "exchange of prisoners." This seems to have settled the matter. Pope John Paul II asked the abductors during his Palm Sunday Angelus that March, "Let them go back to their monastery safe and sound, and let them take up their place again among their Algerian friends."

But his pleas were to no avail. On May 23, Radio Medi I in Tangiers read extracts from a GIA communiqué announcing that they had cut the throats of all seven monks—Dom Christian de Chergè, Brother Luke Dochier, Father Christopher Lebreton, Brother Michael Fleury, Father Bruno Lemarchand, Father Celestine Ringeard, and Brother Paul Favre Miville. That evening, in a powerfully symbolic act watched by millions on television, Cardinal Lustiger of Paris extinguished the seven candles which, in the presence of Christian, Muslim, and Jewish leaders, he had lit seven weeks earlier as a prayer and a hope for the release of the seven monks.

The heads of the monks were left to be found, but not their bodies. The funeral Mass took place in the Algiers Basilica of Our Lady of Africa. Cardinal Arinze, an African himself, presided along with various French, Algerian, and other dignitaries. The remains were then quietly taken, with military security, back to the monastery for burial together in the cemetery there. Many of the Muslim villagers who had loved and received so much from the monks gathered and dug the graves of the seven men just outside the monastic church.

Several Algerians, including the neighbors of the monastery, offered their sincere condolences for the loss of seven men who were both monks and friends to Muslims. In a touching sign that the monk's love for the people of Algeria had been reciprocated, thousands of Algerian Muslims sent letters of regret and apology to Bishop Henri Teissier in Algiers. Muslim leaders elsewhere followed suit, calling the murders "a criminal act contrary to all divine religions," "inhuman," and "outside the bounds of humanity."

Rabah Kebir, the leader of the Islamic Salvation Front, who had earlier demanded of the GIA the release of the seven monks, spoke out most forcefully: "I strongly condemn this criminal act, which runs absolutely contrary to the principles of Islam." Kahdidja Khalil of the High Council of French Muslims went further: "We strongly condemn this savage and barbaric act. It is forbidden in the holy Koran to touch 'all servants of God,' and that means priests and rabbis as well." The High Council had issued a fatwa, a solemn religious decree, declaring the monks' abduction illegal and calling for a day of fasting to pray for their release.

In his address on Pentecost to the faithful in the piazza of St. Peter's, Pope John Paul II said: "Despite our deep sorrow, we thank God for the witness of love given by these religious. Their fidelity and constancy give honor to the church and surely will be seeds of reconciliation and peace for the Algerian people, with whom they were in solidarity."

Also on Pentecost Sunday, in a symbolically powerful gesture once again, Cardinal Lustiger relit the seven candles before the high altar of Notre Dame Cathedral as a sign of reconciliation, declaring that the monks had not died in vain, but rather "for life, for love, and for reconciliation."

• • •

On May 26, 1996, Dom Christian's mother in France opened a sealed letter of her son's last words to the world. The letter on a single handwritten sheet, written earlier by her son Dom Christian, bore the instructions that it be read only in the case of his death. That death had come violently a few days before at the hands of a militant Muslim group: They had beheaded her son on May 21, 1996. In this writing, Christian created a legacy for peace inspired by his monastic spirituality, his sense of living a life that is "GIVEN," and he challenges his readers to a remarkable vision of a living relation between Christians and Muslims.

It reads in part:

When an "A-DIEU" takes on a face.

If it should happen one day—and it could be today—that I become a victim of the terrorism which now seems ready to engulf all the foreigners living in Algeria,

I would like my community, my Church, my family, to remember that my life was GIVEN to God and to this country.

I ask them to accept that the Sole Master of all life was not a stranger to this brutal departure.

I ask them to pray for me—for how could I be found worthy of such an offering?...

My life has no more value than any other. Nor any less value.

In any case it has not the innocence of childhood.

I have lived long enough to know that I am an accomplice in the evil which seems, alas, to prevail in the world, even in that which would strike me blindly.

I should like, when the time comes, to have the moment of lucidity which would allow me to beg forgiveness of God and of my fellow human beings, and at the same time to forgive with all my heart the one who would strike me down.

I could not desire such a death. It seems important to state this.

I do not see, in fact, how I could rejoice if the people I love were to be accused indiscriminately of my murder. To owe it to an Algerian, whoever he may be, would be too high a price to pay for what will, perhaps, be called, the "grace of martyrdom," especially if he says he is acting in fidelity to what he believes to be Islam....

I certainly include you, friends of yesterday and today, and you, my friends of this place, along with my mother and father, my sisters and brothers and their families, the hundredfold granted as was promised!

And also you, the friend of my final moment, who would not be aware of what you were doing. Yes, I also say this THANK YOU and this A-DIEU to you, in whom I see the face of God. And may we find each other, happy good thieves, in Paradise, if it pleases God, the Father of us both. Amen. Insha'Allah.

Algiers, December 1, 1993–Tibhirine, January 1, 1994.

When we look for an end to what some call the continuing clash of civilizations, perhaps we should look less to the negotiations and speeches of political and military leaders but keep an eye to the example of seven modern Christian martyrs.

DISCUSSION QUESTIONS

1. Love of others is central to the message of Christianity. How important is that core message to you, and how do you integrate it into your life?

2. Early in his life in Algiers, as a soldier, Dom Christian's friendship with the Muslim policeman Mohamed changed the course of his life. What "Mohameds" have touched your life in a similar way?

3. As the danger escalated, the monks chose to maintain their neutrality even at the risk of their own lives. Do you think they made the prudent choice? Why or why not?

CHAPTER FIFTEEN

Kneeling on the Fifty-Yard Line
Joe Kennedy

Be strong and bold; have no fear or dread of them, because it is the LORD your God who goes with you; he will not fail you or forsake you.

—Deuteronomy 31:6

His team lost the game. He eventually was suspended from his job as an assistant coach. But there was a great victory that night.

Joe Kennedy had been the assistant head football coach at Bremerton High School in Washington for seven years. After each game, he took a moment to kneel on the fifty-yard line and offer a prayer of thanks for allowing him to play a role in the lives of the young men who played the game. Because for Joe Kennedy, it wasn't just about what the scoreboard said or the X's and O's. It was about the boys learning something about becoming men, about courage, and about working together.

Joe didn't make a big show of his prayer. He wasn't doing it to be seen by others. Maybe that's why he prayed for a while before anyone even took notice.

But then some did.

A few students asked the coach what he was doing. "I was thanking God for you guys," Joe remembered telling his players, according to a Liberty Institute statement. A few of the students asked if they could join him. "It's a free country," he told them. "You can do whatever you want to do."

And he believed it.

Soon some more players on the team noticed and began joining him at the fifty-yard line after the game. He hadn't ordered them. He hadn't even asked them. But they came out to the fifty-yard line and knelt with him after each game for a few moments, win or lose. Sometimes more would join, sometimes less. But those who did joined him because they believed that a prayer was a suitable way to finish a game.

Unsurprisingly to anyone paying attention to twenty-first-century America, irrationality ensued. Fearful of a lawsuit from an atheist group, the school district informed Kennedy that if he didn't stop praying, he would be fired. At first, Kennedy complied. He was surprised. So he didn't pray after the next game.

But that just didn't sit right with the former Marine who'd served in both Operation Desert Storm and Desert Shield. Joe decided he wasn't going to be frightened by a letter or the threat it contained. He told Fox News that he'd put his life on the line to defend the Constitution and wasn't sure that he gave up those rights just because he worked for a public school.

For him, it just came down to the simple question: What would backing down teach his players? "How do you teach your kids about courage if you don't do it?" he told reporters. "I tell my kids to be bold in their beliefs. I want to set an example to stand up for what you believe in, even if it isn't popular."

Kennedy contacted the Liberty Institute, a legal advocacy firm which provides pro bono legal assistance to people of faith and organizations suffering religious persecution in the United States. After a lifetime of standing up for his country, Coach Kennedy decided to kneel down for his beliefs. For decades now, lawyers and government officials have been shrinking the definition of freedom of religion in an effort to ban Christianity from the public sphere. And Joe Kennedy had had enough.

In October of 2015, after a close loss, Kennedy walked alone out to the middle of the field. He knelt, closed his eyes, and prayed. Then he heard some movement beside him.

"All of a sudden I feel all these bodies around me and I'm hoping they're not kids," he later told reporters. He didn't want them to get into trouble. He opened his eyes and saw not only students from his team, but from the other team as well, and a crowd of bystanders from the bleachers. They came out to stand with Joe. They came out to pray before God. They came out to say "enough" to having to back down when confronted by those with radical agendas.

Joe held up the helmets of the two teams which had competed on the field that day and prayed a simple prayer. "Lord, I thank you for these kids and the blessing you've given me with them. We believe in the game, we believe in competition, and we can come in to it as rivals and leave as brothers."

One senior at Bremerton High School told the *Seattle Times*, "It's ridiculous that he got in trouble at all."

Kennedy never saw this fight coming. "I'm not a preachy guy," he said. But this wasn't a fight he was going to walk away from.

• • •

Kennedy vowed to continue with his prayers, and soon his little prayer became a national story with top newspapers filing reports, editorials lambasting and praising Kennedy were circulated, and even the national morning shows featured his story.

The Congressional Prayer Caucus wrote a letter to the Bremerton (Washington) School District arguing that Kennedy had not violated the Establishment Clause of the First Amendment.

"Among the most basic rights that Americans enjoy are the free exercise of religion, free speech, and the freedom of association," wrote Republican caucus cochairmen Senator James Lankford and Representative Randy Forbes.

So intense was the story that even the Satanists got involved. The Satanic Temple of Seattle announced that it would offer its own "services" to anyone at Bremerton who would like to attend a postgame satanic prayer. "We're offering to provide a Satanic invocation for any student or staff member who wishes it," said Lilith Starr of the Satanic Temple of Seattle. They argued that because the school district wasn't doing enough to stop Kennedy from praying, they should not be allowed to prevent a satanic prayer.

On October 23, Superintendent Leavell sent yet another letter to Kennedy. This time, he said, according to Fox News, "Any further violations will be grounds for discipline, up to and including discharge from District employment." Leavell did reportedly say that Kennedy could pray, but only if it was "not observable to students or the public."

The State Superintendent Randy Dorn released a statement as well, saying, "School officials are role models; leading a prayer might put a student in an awkward position, even if the prayer is voluntary.... For students who don't share the official's faith, an official's public expression of faith can seem exclusionary or even distressing."

Kennedy reportedly said that he was shocked. "All I wanted to do was pray," he told Todd Starnes of Fox News. Kennedy vowed to continue praying after each game.

And finally, it happened. Coach Joe Kennedy was put on administrative leave from his position as assistant coach. "Effective immediately, pending further District review of your conduct, you are placed on paid administrative leave from your position as an assistant coach with the Bremerton High School football program," Leavell wrote to the coach in a letter dated October 28. "You may not participate, in any capacity, in BHS football program activities."

For the game on October 29, Joe urged people on his Facebook page to "forget me and come support these incredible young men." He stood in the stands as the team gathered in the locker room. Before the game, many of the players came out to hug the man they still called coach.

And Joe continued to stand there even as a small group of self-described Satanists in black robes showed up to the game but left after all the media had gotten their shots of them. After the game, Joe knelt down to pray at the foot of the bleachers with a group of people who all shouted "Amen" when he finished.

• • •

The history of Christianity is one of seemingly endless defeats transformed by God's grace into glory. Christ died for our sins. The apostles despaired. But Christ rose from the dead, and many of those same apostles were killed after years of preaching, and their deaths caused even greater interest and fidelity to the faith.

One can see Kennedy being suspended from his job as the end of the story, but I think that misses the point. He fights on, not just for himself but for others' right to be Christians. "I'm willing to take this as far as it goes to defend the rights of the Constitution to the end," he said. "If it comes back one way or another, I fought the good fight."

In December of 2015, the Liberty Institute, on behalf of Kennedy, filed a complaint with the US Equal Employment Opportunity Commission for the school's violation of Title VII of the Civil Rights Act of 1964.

Joe Kennedy remembers that his goal as a football coach was to prepare those young men for life, to teach them courage, to teach them how to stand up for themselves. I think he did that. Joe Kennedy may have lost much, but he gained the greater victory.

Discussion Questions

1. How far does the separation of Church and state prevent school district employees from praying? Have there been stories similar to Kennedy's in your area?
2. Do you think being a good role model is synonymous with being a good Christian?
3. Would you stand up for your faith even if it could cost you your job? Under what circumstances?

CHAPTER SIXTEEN

Miracle Gianna
Jessica Chominski

For you have delivered my soul from death,
and my feet from falling,
so that I may walk before God
in the light of life.

—Psalm 56:13

There are currently over two thousand crisis pregnancy
centers in the United States working to remind us all
that every life is sacred. The work they do ministering to
women is, I believe, often a reflection of God's love of all and essentially midwifing miracles by aiding young mothers. Their work is
often overlooked, and this is just one of thousands of stories which
could be told.

Jessica Chominski fights for the lives of others. Little lives. The
ones many don't think are worth fighting for. She was the sole fulltime employee of the Bucks County Community Women's Center,
a crisis pregnancy center in Pennsylvania.

In her interview with me for this book, Jessica explained that
often when a woman makes a decision for life, it's not a one-time
decision. It's a decision made dozens of times. Maybe more. Any
difficulty can make the woman make and remake her decision.
Jessica simply tries to be there to guide.

• • •

About once a week a woman calls or walks into the center asking about abortion, and Jessica asks them why they feel the need to abort their child, she tells them about other options, explains what abortion is, and tells them about the dignity of every human life. "Hopefully they leave thinking twice," she says.

It's nerve-racking work. At twenty-four years old, Jessica works daily under the weight that lives depend on her. Every phone call. Every conversation. And she knows that she can't control what a woman does when she walks out of the center, so she just gives all she can. And when there's no more she can do, she prays. But to her, it's all worth it because, in the end, Jessica knows, "there are babies crawling around right now because of the work we do. And that is miraculous."

It usually starts with a phone call. Jessica knows that every time the phone rings, a life might depend on her. She simply answers the call.

She had no way of knowing that *this* particular call would change her life forever. "Do you guys help out with abortion?" a woman nervously asked.

Jessica informed the woman that they didn't perform abortions at the center. She offered to discuss options. "We can provide information," she said. "Would you like to come by?"

Silence.

Jessica understood what was at stake in that silence. She prayed as she waited for a response. She heard breathing. But she knew that, as long as the woman stayed on the phone, there was hope. She knew what a sudden dial tone would likely mean. She listened to the breathing on the other end of the line until she heard a barely breathed, "OK."

When meeting with a pregnant woman, Jessica says the first thing she tries to understand is why the woman feels an abortion is her only option. When Rebecca (not her real name) came in, she explained she was already a mother of three and her boyfriend, the father of her unborn child, was adamant she have an abortion.

Jessica told Rebecca about fetal development. She talked about adoption. She told her there were other options. But Jessica couldn't tell if she was getting through. And when Rebecca left that day, Jessica's hopes were not high. "I know she was a little unsure," she says.

She didn't hear from Rebecca for weeks. Standard policy for the center is they follow up with two phone calls, but Rebecca didn't answer or return the calls. Jessica thought she'd never hear from Rebecca again.

Weeks later, a cousin of Rebecca's—a former client of the center who'd considered abortion but eventually chose life—brought Rebecca back to the center because she was trying to talk her out of aborting her child.

Rebecca and Jessica spoke for hours. Rebecca told her about her boyfriend's abuse and her estranged relationship with her religious mother. And how she felt she had nowhere to turn. And that started a period of two months in which Rebecca vacillated back and forth on whether to abort. At one point, Rebecca actually scheduled an abortion for the following Friday at a local abortion clinic in nearby Warminster. That week, Jessica was on pins and needles.

The two women spoke often. Jessica could just be there for her, a voice urging life. Volunteers at the clinic babysat her children while they spoke. Jessica says,

> When she had scheduled the appointment...I initiated my prayer-chain of family and friends. I emailed about forty people at first, but the story ended up spreading literally across the country. These people were amazing—they did novenas, they fasted, they prayed, a bunch of priest friends

offered Masses, I contacted a few deeply prayerful orders of religious sisters, and we stormed the heavens for four days. Local parishioners offered to be at the clinic. The prayer support was astronomical. That is why she didn't have the abortion on Friday.

Just to make sure, though, Jessica gave Rebecca and her cousin grocery cards to keep her away from the clinic all day while she babysat both their kids. But she insists it was the prayers that did it.

Rebecca didn't keep the appointment at the Planned Parenthood clinic that Friday. And finally Rebecca told Jessica that she chose to keep the baby. "We all breathed a sigh of relief," she says. "It had been such a long process, but she made a decision for life."

• • •

The relief would be short-lived. When Rebecca's boyfriend learned of her decision, he repeatedly and savagely kicked her in the stomach. While examining her, hospital doctors said they saw something alarming. There was no amniotic fluid, which would likely cause the baby's lungs to not develop properly.

Jessica and Rebecca decided to have the baby checked out together at St. Mary's Medical Center, a Catholic hospital in Langhorne, Pennsylvania. Jessica was worried about the baby, but she was also worried about how Rebecca would take any news. *Would she consider aborting the baby again?* she wondered.

The appointment they headed to that day would surely be a difficult one. "But I was excited she was going to a Catholic hospital," says Jessica. "I thought this will be difficult, but at least they'll have compassion for life of the baby."

Rebecca, at eighteen weeks pregnant, had an ultrasound done. The two women held hands while waiting together. Unfortunately, after the ultrasound, the doctor had some terrible news. The baby was sick. Very sick. The baby was also diagnosed with polycystic kidneys—a fatal disease that assured the baby likely wouldn't make it to term and would most assuredly die shortly after birth from its underdeveloped lungs.

And then it happened.

While the women wept together, the doctor coolly added that he could schedule a "termination" because there was no reason Rebecca should go through a pregnancy and deliver a child since it would die almost immediately after.

Jessica couldn't believe what she was hearing. "The worst part is he just told her that her baby was going to die, and we're both crying. And the next thing out of his mouth was termination. I said, 'We are in a Catholic hospital.' I probably looked pretty angry," said Jessica. "And he said, 'I know, but she can come over to my office in Abington.'"

Abortion was back on the table.... After months of working with the baby's mother to help her choose life, the doctor at the Catholic hospital "kicked back all the work we'd done."

"I was devastated," Jessica says. She was also frustrated, disappointed, and infuriated that this doctor would suggest such a thing at a Catholic hospital. "We were backtracked to where we'd been in June," she said. "It just seemed that there was no safe harbor for this child. This poor little sheep had no shepherd."

Jessica knew that if she hadn't been sitting right there next to Rebecca, the pregnancy likely would've ended in an abortion. She said so many people seek out Catholic hospitals because "they believe that they'll respect the dignity of the person. And when recommendations such as abortion come from a Catholic institution, people accept it. There's so much authority there."

• • •

According to their own website, the hospital insists that it follows the Ethical and Religious Directives for Catholic Health Care Services. However, the United States Conference of Catholic Bishops (USCCB) guidelines state, "First, Catholic health care ministry is rooted in a commitment to promote and defend human dignity; this is the foundation of its concern to respect the sacredness of every human life from the moment of conception until death."

Further along, the USCCB states that "employees of a Catholic health care institution must respect and uphold the religious mission of the institution." That, of course, would preclude abortion, but here's how those rules seem to be gotten around.

Lester A. Ruppersberger, DO, a pro-life gynecologist formerly on staff at St. Mary's, now on staff at the Center for Women's Health in Langhorne, says a doctor at a Catholic hospital recommending abortion is hardly an anomaly. He says that Catholic hospitals cannot turn away doctors from renting space in their medical offices, that while doctors may not perform procedures like abortion in the hospital, administrators "draw a line" between where the hospital ends and the medical office building begins.

"They'll say they can't control the philosophy of the people who are renting from their medical office building; they can't tell them what to do in their private practice," he says. "You can have the world's number one abortionist at a Catholic hospital. They can't legally keep him off staff." So doctors affiliated with St. Mary's actually dispense contraception and can have abortions performed in another building.

John Stanton of the Pro-Life Union of Southeastern Pennsylvania says, "The people who run the hospital make a point of saying that he's not going to do it at the hospital. So somehow it becomes not an objective evil because it's not done there? It's wrong to kill a baby here but somewhere else it's OK?"

• • •

Jessica had worried that after what happened at St. Mary's Hospital, Rebecca only needed the slightest push in order to abort, so she accompanied Rebecca to almost all of her prenatal visits. She says they were all the same, even those at the Catholic hospital. "She'd leave these prenatal visits crying because these doctors would make her feel so guilty that she wasn't going to kill her baby. I had to yell at some doctors. I feel really bad about it, but I had to."

Rebecca went to four hospitals, and all of them didn't just recommend abortion, Jessica says, "They shoved it down her throat."

It got so bad that Rebecca was often too frightened to ask questions herself for fear she'd be berated for not aborting her child. So Rebecca would give Jessica questions in the car for her to ask. Rebecca was hardly able to look up at the doctors.

When Rebecca was twenty weeks along, she went to a secular hospital in Philadelphia. Jessica couldn't make that visit, but Rebecca assured her it would be all right.

But it wasn't. From the hospital, Rebecca called to tell Jessica the hospital was sending her to have labor induced. Rebecca had specifically told the medical staff that she didn't want an abortion, but they told her that she could deliver the baby then and would be allowed to hold her baby, giving what they called "comfort care," and say good-bye.

"That's an abortion," said Jessica.

"No," said Rebecca. "The doctors said it wasn't."

"Your baby will not have a fighting chance," explained Jessica. "Your baby couldn't possibly survive right now."

When Jessica hung up the phone, she had no idea what would happen. Rebecca, still unsure, had her mind made up when the hospital asked her to sign autopsy papers for research purposes. "She was horrified," says Jessica. "Autopsy papers?"

Rebecca finally told the doctors that she wanted God to decide when this baby would be taken. Not her. Not the doctors. Nobody but God.

"I was so proud of her for that," says Jessica. "That was such a beautiful moment."

· · ·

Just when it seemed that nobody could quite see a reason that the baby should be born, Rebecca had found the strength to stand up for her baby. Rebecca was affirmed in her faith by a surprising source. She read a piece online by Father John Zuhlsdorf concerning the second miracle attributed to St. Gianna, about a mother with no amniotic fluid giving birth to a beautiful baby girl after doctors had recommended an abortion.

Rebecca became fascinated by St. Gianna and her amazing example of motherhood. At one point, Rebecca was even visited by members of the Society of St. Gianna, who laid the glove of St. Gianna on Rebecca's womb. "She was so touched by these people who didn't even know her, affirming her, how they were praying for her, and their empathy," says Jessica.

Rebecca began attending Mass again with her mother, the experience moving her in her faith. And shortly after, Rebecca even asked doctors for a "super-hydration" injection she'd read about in Fr. Zuhlsdorf's article to help the baby's lungs. This woman who'd been too afraid to open her mouth in doctors' offices weeks before was now demanding that everything be done to save her baby. Medical staff were surprised and wondered aloud how she even knew about the injection. They attempted to dissuade her, but she insisted.

Rebecca was fighting for her baby.

Jessica got the call on January 9 that the baby was coming, and she rushed to Abington Hospital. Rebecca had asked Jessica to stay in the delivery room with her. Moments before the baby was born, Jessica pulled the doctor aside and told him, "You promise her that you're going to treat her baby like you're treating your own daughter?"

The doctor promised.

When the baby was born, there were no cries from the baby. The child never even opened her eyes. Her little lungs struggled for each gasping breath. It was apparent to all that the baby wouldn't live long.

The nurses handed the baby to Jessica. She looked at the beautiful baby in her arms, and for a few moments she couldn't be sad. She held the precious little life in her arms. "I took her over, and she met her mom, and it was absolutely beautiful," says Jessica. "The anesthesiologist was crying. Everyone was totally blown away. She lived for about an hour and a half."

There wasn't time to figure out if she had her mother's hair or her grandmother's nose. She had a soul that belonged to God that it seems just couldn't stand being away from his presence for even a day.

Rebecca, still on the surgical table and groggy from the pain medication, gave Jessica a job: Make sure the baby is baptized. "That was my one mission," says Jessica. "And it's really the best mission."

> I was like a pitbull in that delivery room. I told them they had to find a priest to come in there, and they were so confused. When I said "priest," the nurses must have heard "nondenominational clergy-person who believes in God" because in came this guy who thought he was baptizing the mother and was extremely confused when I explained exactly how he needed to perform an infant baptism. I had called my friend, Fr. Kevin McGoldrick, on the way to the hospital, and he had given me the correct formula for the baptism.

Just as the baptism was to take place, a nurse ran out of the room and came back with a little white dress, booties, and a hat for the little baby's baptism. "There wasn't a dry eye there," said Jessica.

The baby was baptized "Miracle Gianna."

"It was an honor to be there. A witness of God's mercy. And they all treated this baby like a person," says Jessica. "And she died with Christ, and as tragic as it was it, was the most beautiful thing we could've asked for. Now the baby's in heaven."

The nurse pulled Jessica aside and told her that she'd go to Church on Sunday and pray for little baby Gianna. Jessica told her that baby Gianna would be praying for her as well.

Baby Gianna had finally found her safe harbor. For so long, Jessica had worried that this little lost sheep was without a shepherd, but that day, little baby Gianna found her eternal home in the arms of Christ the Shepherd.

Baby Gianna had a mother who fought for her and a God who loved her. "As a parent, it's your job to get your child to heaven," says Jessica. "That is what parenthood is supposed to be. And she did it."

After the funeral, Jessica asked Rebecca if it was all worth it. Rebecca looked her friend in the eye and told her, "I know I did the right thing. I would do it all over again."

Nine months and ninety minutes changed everything for so many. Jessica says, "This baby moved mountains. Brought me closer to God. Brought her mother closer to God."

And little Gianna's life may have had more of an impact than anyone in the room that day could've realized.

• • •

Because of what occurred in the Catholic hospital, many pro-life organizations are focusing on Catholic hospitals upholding Catholic principles.

The *Philadelphia Bulletin* ran a story concerning the doctor's recommendation of an abortion at St. Mary's, a Catholic hospital. That article has begun a firestorm of criticism. John Stanton, Public Affairs of the Pro-Life Union of Southeastern Pennsylvania says, "This one burned. This isn't going away." He says, "This baby's creation and death is not going to go away. Some good will come of this. I can tell you that."

Jessica Chominski delivered this eulogy for Baby Miracle Gianna:

On January 9, the world changed forever because of a baby girl. I know that many of you do not know the whole story of Miracle Gianna. Many of you have been praying for her fervently—praying for her to heal, praying for her to be OK, praying for her to live.

We have all had a piece of this story, which on the outside, looks like a tragic, sad, devastating defeat. But this is not a story of defeat. This is a story of triumph—the triumph of baptism.

When she was born, the doctors handed her to me to hold, and I have never felt more humbled and fearful in my life. I was not afraid because her precious, beautiful body was so fragile and delicate, but because I knew that I was standing in the presence of a little girl who would soon be in heaven with Our Lord. I didn't know how long we would get to be with her, but I knew that she was going from my arms and the arms of her loving, brave mother to the arms of Our Lady, who would take her home to her Son. I knew that in a few hours or a few moments, while we sat weeping, the angels would be singing her lullabies as she rested in the comfort of her Creator. This was because of an act of heroic motherhood.

Rebecca spent the last four months hoping and praying that her baby girl would live. Up until the moment we went into the delivery room, she did not abandon this hope, despite the definitive prognosis. As she realized that God had greater plans for her baby, in a moment of what appeared to be defeat, she did not buckle. She insisted that Miracle be given eternity—she insisted that she was baptized.

It was in this moment that we witnessed the triumph of the resurrection. Just as Our Lady held the broken body of her Son, her Savior as he was taken from the cross, trusting that

He would rise in three days as he had promised, so too did Rebecca hold her baby, trusting in the promise of Our Lord to his Church. She lives in eternity now because her mother did what parents are supposed to do—she got her child to heaven.

Jessica says that it was no coincidence that this long, difficult story came to its conclusion on the Feast of the Baptism of Our Lord.

As I drove home from the hospital, that night, well, that morning, I was listening to music on my iPod, trying to be a good driver as I was holding back sobs. On came "How Great Thou Art," one of my favorite songs, but one that almost seemed ironically inappropriate at a time like this. But as I listened to the words of the song, I realized that the same Creator that fashioned the heavens, the earth, the vastness of the universe, also fashioned this little girl's tiny hands, feet, adorable button nose, and perfectly coiffed hair. He had breathed his life into her, then she rose to new life with him, and it was for this reason that her life was worth so much—so that we could look at her and exclaim, "My God, how great Thou art!"

Miracle Gianna, pray for us.

The following day, Jessica was back answering phones and counseling women.

DISCUSSION QUESTIONS

1. The work of crisis pregnancy centers is amazing. What could you be doing to help a local center near you?

2. What would you say to encourage a pregnant woman who had been counseled to abort her child because of a difficult prenatal diagnosis?

3. How did little Gianna, in her short time on earth, make a difference?

CHAPTER SEVENTEEN

The Wedding Cake
Jack Phillips

I hereby command you: Be strong and courageous; do not
be frightened or dismayed, for the LORD your God is with
you wherever you go.

—Joshua 1:9

I
t's likely you've heard or read about a baker who refused to bake
a cake for a same-sex wedding. You've probably heard or read
all sorts of accusations against the baker being "homophobic"
or a "hater," but none of those words apply to Jack Phillips.

What interested me about Jack is how it seems quite likely that
he'll lose everything he's ever worked for because of his faith. I
spoke to Jack at length, and what amazed me about him is that
despite everything, this is a man in love with God who's willing to
stand up to everything the world could throw at him for his faith.

• • •

When Jack Phillips graduated high school, he needed a job. It was
as simple as that. So he stopped in to a local bakery and asked
if they needed help. They hired him, and he discovered he truly
enjoyed the work.

Jack Phillips was a baker.

Working nights at the bakery, he and a few others would usually
go to the bar after their shift. "And then one particular day I
didn't," he explains. "I believe the Holy Spirit came into the car

and convicted me of my sins, and I knew he was right. I was a sinner."

He knew that as Romans says, "the wages of sin is death" and that Christ died for all of our sins. He knew he couldn't clean up his life on his own and said, "I'm yours."

Jack Phillips was a Christian. It was as simple as that.

It was the American dream. A small bakery shop owned by a good Christian man with a bushy beard and a winning smile. His mother volunteered a few times a week to handle accounts payable. He was closed on Sundays.

Jack Phillips, a married man for almost forty years and a father of three grown children, loved waking up in the morning to do what he did. He has said he can't remember a day when he didn't want to come to work. "I enjoy every aspect of it," he told me. "Baking, washing dishes, cleaning floors. I enjoy it."

Jack especially enjoyed designing and creating wedding cakes. He considered himself a "cake artist" and loved making original creations for the couples who came in. He estimates he made about two hundred wedding cakes per year. "It's getting to know them for first time. It's about making lifelong friends and customers," he says. "A wedding is a special event. It's usually the biggest day of their life, especially the bride's. To get everything right and be a part of that is really a cool thing."

• • •

It was the American dream. But America was changing. And change came in the door of the Masterpiece Cakeshop when two men walked in and asked for a wedding cake.

He said, "Hi, guys."

They introduced themselves, and Jack said, "What can I do for you?'

"We're here to look at wedding cakes," one said. The other quickly added, "Yeah, and it's for our wedding."

Jack said, "Sorry, guys, I don't make cakes for same-sex weddings."

"What?" they asked.

"I'll make you birthday cakes, shower cakes, sell you cookies or brownies, but I just don't do cakes for same-sex weddings," Jack said. He also didn't make Halloween cakes. He felt that, too, was against his faith. But he didn't get a chance to explain to them about his faith. He didn't get a chance to say anything because the two men went toward the door, but not before one of them turned and said, "F— you and your f—ing homophobic cake shop," and flipped him off.

And then they were gone. The whole interaction was no more than thirty seconds long. But Jack's world was changed forever, even though he didn't know it.

He thought the unpleasantness was over. That is, until the phones started ringing. It was people yelling the worst possible things at him. And the calls kept coming. And there was even one very specific death threat.

One eerie caller told Jack he was going to come to the shop and shoot him. He said he was close by, close enough to know that Jack's daughter was in the shop.

"It was disconcerting because my daughter and granddaughter were here at the time. He was saying he'd come over and shoot me. I told my daughter to take my granddaughter to the back, and I called the police."

He explained everything to the police, and the man even called back when the police were there, but they failed to learn the caller's identity.

Shortly after, the two men filed a complaint with the Colorado Civil Rights Commission and were represented by the American Civil Liberties Union.

The Civil Rights Commission (CRC) ordered Jack and his staff to make cakes for same-sex celebrations. He was also ordered to reeducate his staff about Colorado's Anti-Discrimination Act and submit quarterly "compliance" reports to the government for two years.

One of the commissioners reportedly compared Jack to a slave owner or a participant in the Holocaust, saying, just prior to denying Jack's request to temporarily suspend the commission's reeducation order, "Freedom of religion and religion have been used to justify all kinds of discrimination throughout history, whether it be slavery, whether it be the Holocaust.... I mean, we can list hundreds of situations where freedom of religion has been used to justify discrimination. And to me it is one of the most despicable pieces of rhetoric that people can use—to use their religion to hurt others."

At that point, given the commissioner's decision, Jack decided to simply refuse to bake any wedding cakes at all. He knew it would hurt his business terribly. At that time, wedding cakes were about 40 percent of his business. But he never doubted that what he was doing was the right thing. "I rely on my faith every day. I trust that Jesus Christ is my Lord and Savior," he said. "We were not going to do same-sex [wedding] cakes. Still won't. No plans to change our mind."

Nicolle Martin, the lead attorney who took on Jack's case pro bono and is affiliated with the Alliance Defending Freedom (ADF), said, "All I can say is what that looks like to me is something very frightening, and that's nothing more than diversity through conformity, and that's not diversity at all."

In a puzzling hypocrisy, another similar case was brought before the Colorado Civil Rights Commission by a Christian who was turned away by three bakeries when he asked them to bake cakes decorated with Bible verses affirming traditional marriage. The

CRC interestingly exonerated those three bakeries.

The ADF commended the CRC for that decision, saying "cake artists should not be forced to violate their conscience." But the fact that the commission sided with them and not Jack is "inconsistent," they said.

The ADF called the hypocrisy "blatant religious discrimination." Ironically, the ACLU, in that case, sided with the bakers.

Unfortunately, Jack, though not forced to lay any of his employees off, wasn't able to replace any workers who left. His mother helps out more and jokes frequently about being sent to reeducation camp. His sister also helps out when she can. They're proud of Jack and the decision he's made.

And a funny thing happened. Some in the area who support him come in more frequently to buy cakes or brownies, maybe even more than they need. They want to show their support, and Jack is grateful for it. Other strangers simply send in donations to help.

Jack took the case to court arguing for freedom of speech, but in December 2013, Colorado Judge Robert Spencer ruled that Jack's actions were not protected by the Constitution's guaranteed freedom of speech. The judge pointed out that the cake didn't explicitly include text supporting "gay marriage."

The judge in the case also ruled that Jack had no right to live out his religious beliefs in his business, saying that baking a wedding cake "does not involve an effort by the government to regulate what respondents believe. Rather, it involves that state's regulation of conduct."

In short, Jack was once again ordered to bake wedding cakes for same-sex marriages.

He could've ended it there. He could've said he tried to fight it, but the courts ruled. He knew that continuing to fight could mean his financial ruination. It could mean the closing of his shop. He knew that ending it there might even be the smart play.

Instead, he appealed the decision to the Colorado Supreme Court with the help of Nicolle and the ADF. Together, they argued that Jack didn't refuse the cake because of the couple's sex orientation, as he had served many homosexuals in the past. In fact, he'd specifically said he would bake anything but a wedding cake for them because his faith prohibits him from affirming gay marriage ceremonies through his actions.

They argued that Jack, as an artist, should be able to choose to promote certain events or not to, as the case may be. The petition, in part, states:

> Phillips...honors God through his creative work by declining to use his artistic talents to design and create cakes that violate his religious beliefs.... This includes cakes with offensive written messages and cakes celebrating events or ideas that violate his beliefs, including cakes celebrating Halloween, anti-American or anti-family themes, atheism, racism, or indecency.... He also will not create cakes with hateful, vulgar, or profane messages, or sell any products containing alcohol.... Consistent with this longtime practice, Phillips also will not create cakes celebrating any marriage that is contrary to biblical teaching.

Jack Phillips is a baker. Jack Phillips is a Christian. He doesn't believe he has to stop being a Christian the moment he opens the doors of his bakery.

He doesn't know what the future will bring. He knows that he won't be baking any cakes for a same-sex wedding. And he knows that whatever the state does to him, God will provide. That, he knows. It's as simple as that.

DISCUSSION QUESTIONS

1. Jack Phillips honors God through his work. Can you think of ways you honor God through your work?

2. Jack Phillips could possibly lose everything because of his fidelity to his faith. Have you ever risked something for your faith? How did you get through it?

3. How does the Catholic understanding of tolerance differ from that of general secular culture? (See CCC 1740).

CHAPTER EIGHTEEN

Losing All, but Not Everything

Kanaka Rekha Nayak

He called the crowd with his disciples, and said to them, "If any want to become my followers, let them deny themselves and take up their cross and follow me. For those who want to save their life will lose it, and those who lose their life for my sake, and for the sake of the gospel, will save it. For what will it profit them to gain the whole world and forfeit their life? Indeed, what can they give in return for their life?

—Mark 8:34–38

The murderous persecution of Christians is occurring today in many parts of the globe. While many know of the persecution in the Middle East and in China and in India, the persecution of Christians has sadly become an all too common event. We must pray for the persecuted but also be inspired by them.

• • •

When Kanaka Rekha Nayak first heard the angry crowd entering the village, it must have sounded like a growling and ferocious monster. If only it had been! A monster might have treated her more kindly.

When she heard of the August 24, 2008, assassination of

Lakshmanananda Saraswati, a Hindu religious leader, Kanaka, the Christian wife of Parikhita Nayak, very likely assumed it didn't have anything to do with her. Maoist revolutionaries had claimed responsibility for the attack. But as Saraswati himself had often railed against and denounced the work of Christians among villagers of the low caste who were considered "untouchables," much of his supporter's ire about his death focused squarely on Christians.

An angry mob of about four hundred took to burning and looting over six thousand Christian homes, leaving over fifty thousand Christians homeless. Christian women were sexually assaulted openly, and their attackers suffered little consequence. One elderly nun was raped when attackers robbed the school where she worked. Police essentially stood by as nearly four hundred Christian churches were burned along with dozens of schools.

On the afternoon of August 25, Kanaka was at home with her two young children when she heard the burgeoning shouting. The angry and violent mob had entered her village chanting anti-Christian slogans. With fear and a mother's protective instinct rising, she immediately gathered her two young children and fled the house, seeking shelter in the cover of the wild jungle. Running into the shadows of the jungle, she turned in time to see her home engulfed in flames.

One thought concerned her more than all others—her husband Parikhita Nayak. He had been in a neighboring house, which the angry mob encircled while brandishing axes and knives as well as guns. After a few moments, the house was set ablaze, and her husband emerged along with two of his friends. She saw him pushing through the violent mob and watched as his two friends fell under its feet, where they were tortured, slashed, and cut. Finally, her husband was somehow able to push free to the outer circle and dash into the jungle.

He had escaped. For now.

The horror was not over, however. Homeless, the mother and children laid down in the jungle for the night, then attempted to make it to her mother's home. They stole through the jungle, always careful not to make a sound. When they finally made it to her mother's home, she discovered her husband there. They prayed together and decided that whatever God wanted, his will would be done.

They soon learned it was terribly unsafe there as well, so the family returned to the jungle in order to trek to another distant town where they might find safety, if only for a little while. Eventually, after another day of walking through the jungle, their young daughter cried for water. So they decided to make their way down nearer the road in search of water for their daughter.

As they approached, they were spotted by the murderous anti-Christian horde and taken prisoner. They soon found themselves surrounded by one hundred people waving swords, axes, and guns with deadly intent.

Cursing Parikhita, they dragged him to a nearby temple and tied his hands around a pole. And then the savage beatings began, all the while screaming at him to renounce Christianity and convert to Hinduism. Parikhita simply responded that they may kill him, but he would never renounce his Christianity. "I've known the Lord for thirty years," he said. "I cannot deny the Lord."

This enraged the crowd even further, and the beatings began anew. Kanaka remembers her daughter crying, "Please, leave my dad." Desperate, Kanaka threw herself down at the feet of her husband's torturers begging for mercy. Instead, they wrapped a bicycle chain around his neck and dragged him about a kilometer to a public square, all the while savagely slashing at him with their swords and knives. According to reports, they cut off his genitals and tore out his intestines and wore them around their necks as prizes of the slaughter. Finally, they cut his throat, covered him in kerosene, and burned him.

As the crowd turned back toward Kanaka, she grabbed her two children and escaped back into the jungle. The following morning, Kanaka ran with her two children to the police station in nearby Raikia, a relief camp, and told them everything that had happened. But by the time they returned to the scene of the crime, the mob had buried Parikhita's body and dispersed. Kanaka was eventually able to recover her husband's body and bury him properly, and some of those responsible for his murder were later arrested.

Kanaka offered her witness at the National Eucharistic Congress in November 2015 in Mumbai. The archbishop of Bombay, Cardinal Oswald Gracias, has recently requested that the Church in India initiate proceedings to possibly declare those lost to anti-Christian violence in India as martyrs to the faith. "I have spoken to the Prefect of the Pontifical Congregation of the Causes of Martyrs in Rome," he reportedly said. "I am willing to speak personally about Kandhamal violence and its martyrs to Pope Francis, whenever there is an opportunity."

The horrors that occurred throughout those four months in Kandhamal claimed nearly one hundred lives. Because so many were still afraid of the attackers, there was a lack of witness testimony in the trial against the murderers. And after serving about seven years in prison, the men who slaughtered Kanaka's husband are free today. She sees them often, and they continue to openly threaten her life along with the lives of her children. According to the organization Speak Out Against Hate, Christians in India even today face "unprecedented violence and discrimination," which often goes unreported for fear of reprisal.

Despite the threats and violence, Kanaka refuses to be swayed in her faith. "I have lost my husband, my home and properties," she told the National Eucharistic Congress, "but I have not lost my faith. Jesus is my Savior."

Discussion Questions

1. Church history is full of stories of men and women who withstood great suffering and torture rather than renouncing their faith. Which of these stories are most meaningful to you, and why?

2. The word *martyr* means "witness." The *Catechism* defines martyrdom as follows: "*Martyrdom* is the supreme witness given to the truth of the faith: it means bearing witness even unto death. The martyr bears witness to Christ who died and rose, to whom he is united by charity. He bears witness to the truth of the faith and of Christian doctrine. He endures death through an act of fortitude" (CCC 2473). What is the difference, then, between a murder and a martyrdom?

3. How has your faith supported you in times of tragedy?

CONCLUSION

Storytelling is at the heart of Christianity. We study and discuss the life, death, and resurrection of Christ in the Gospels. We read and are inspired by the histories of saints. Jesus himself spoke in parables to teach us the lessons of love, forgiveness, and sacrifice.

This is no mistake. Because Christianity, at its heart, is not a religion best understood through its laws and prohibitions but through stories of humans living the Gospel. In fact, the way the Gospels were spread for generations was through the oral tradition of stories.

It is one thing to be instructed to love one's neighbor, but reading about the Good Samaritan makes the message resonate. When Jesus attempted to teach Peter about forgiveness, he told him not to forgive just seven times but "seventy times seven."

So after attempting to get his lead apostle to do heavy math without a calculator or an abacus handy, he quickly followed with a story with a king seeking to settle accounts with his servants. The one servant owed the king a great deal and begged for mercy and was forgiven his debt. But then that same servant brutalized another who owed him a much lesser sum. Because of that the king had him thrown in jail.

Surely, this is a way to draw the listener into a story and identify more readily with the message. As long as there are Christians, there will be stories. Stories can educate, inspire, and build communities.

The stories in this book are extraordinary tales of ordinary

Christians. There are thousands of stories like them out in the world. Anonymous Christians live out their faith in the face of persecution on every continent. Their stories often go ignored by the mainstream media. Their efforts deserve our recognition, and their souls require our prayers.

Those who shelter the homeless, love the stranger, and aid the needy deserve our support, and those who steadfastly proclaim the sanctity of life and the sacramentality of marriage need our prayers. Together we should support them, pray for them, and tell their stories.

ACKNOWLEDGMENTS

Thank you to Jill Stanek, Baronelle Stutzman, Dr. Phillip Hawley Jr., Jack Phillips, Dr. George Isajiw, Heather Mercer, Naghmeh Abedini, Thomas Geromichalos, and others for speaking with me about these stories. You are all truly an inspiration.

Thank you to my wife, Christie, and my children Mary Cate, Corinne, Shannon, Connor, and Bridget for allowing me to make those phone calls and bury my nose in a computer for hours at a time.

Thank you to the editorial staff at Servant and Franciscan Media for putting up with me.

CHAPTER ONE: *Angels atop Schoolhouses*

Bovsun, Mara. "Mystery Still Surrounds Charles Carl Roberts' 2006 Murderous Rampage in West Nickels Mine, Pa.," *New York Daily News*, August 23, 2014.

Cannarsa, Andrew. "Hundreds of Amish Turn Out for First Funerals in Schoolhouse Shooting," *The Phoenix Reporter and Item*, October 6, 2006.

Dribben, Melissa. "In Amish Survivor's Baby, Hope Lives 'Shattered, but Strong': Woman who escaped death relates her story," *Philadelphia Inquirer*, October 22, 2006.

Fisher, Suzanne. "Plain Talk about the Amish: The Comfort Quilt," *Amish Principles for Today's Families*, blog at Christian Post. July 26, 2012.

Itkowitz, Colby. "Teacher's Escape Saved Pupils' Lives," Lancaster Online. October 4, 2006.

Jackson, Peter. "3 Girls in Attack Go Back to Amish school," *Seattle Times*, November 21, 2006.

Jones, Tamara, and Joshua Partlow. "Death Toll in Attack at Amish School Rises to 5," *Washington Post*, October 4, 2006.

Journal Register News Service. "Amish Community Mourns," *The Trentonian*, October 6, 2006.

King, Larry, Emilie Lounsberry, and Natalie Pompilio. "'I just took, uh, 10 girls hostage and I want everybody off the property...or else.' On 911 Tape, Roberts Warns Police to Leave Scene, 'or else' Amish Shootings: The 911 Tapes," *Philadelphia Inquirer*, October 11, 2006.

Kocieniewki, David, and Shaila Dewan. "Elaborate Plan Seen by Police in School Siege," *New York Times*, October 4, 2006.

Kocieniewki, David, and Gary Gately. "Man Shoots 11, Killing 5 Girls, in Amish School," *New York Times*, October 3, 2006.

Miller, Meg. "Comfort Quilt Helps Heal Community," *Collegiate Times*, August 22, 2007.

Satauffer, Cindy, and Ad Crable. "Exclusive: Interview with Slain Amish Girls' Families," Lancaster Online. September 16, 2007.

CHAPTER TWO: *The Triumph over Emptiness*
Carroll, Rory, "Girls Confess to Killing Nun 'for sport,'" *The Guardian*, June 30, 2000.

Catholic News Agency. "Pope Speaks about Religious Sister Who Was Killed by Satanists," April 9, 2008. http://www.catholic-newsagency.com/news/pope_speaks_about_religious_sister_who_was_killed_by_satanists/.

EWTN. "Rock Music Plays Role in Nun's Murder in Italy," A Zenit Daily Dispatch. July 11, 2000. https://www.ewtn.com/library/ISSUES/ZVIROCK.HTM.

Magister, Sandro. "From Black Masses to Black Metal: The Last Temptation of Satan," Chiesa Espress Online. http://chiesa.espresso.repubblica.it/articolo/7046?eng=y&refresh_ce.

Manzari, Claudio. "Le assassine: la suora doveva morire Confessano tre ragazze di 17 anni: "Era un gioco, poi l'abbiamo uccisa," *Violenza Donne*. June 30, 2000.

Zenit. "Cause Opens for Religious Slain in Satanic Rite," November 6, 2005. http://www.zenit.org/en/articles/cause-opens-for-religious-slain-in-satanic-rite.

CHAPTER THREE: *The Hardest to Forgive*
Adair, Catherine. "Planned Parenthood lies about itself," *Washington Examiner*, November 22, 2011.

CHAPTER FOUR: *Love That Liberates*
Jordan, Mary, and Kevin Sullivan. "The Prison Angel: Mother Antonia's Journey from Beverly Hills to a Life of Service in a Mexican Jail," New York: Penguin, 2006.

Schudel, Matt. "Mother Antonia, 86, Brought Comfort to Inmates of a Notorious Mexican Prison," *Washington Post*, October 19, 2013.

Yardley, William. "Antonia Brenner, 'Prison Angel' Who Took Inmates Under Her Wing, Is Dead at 86," *New York Times*, October 20, 2013.

CHAPTER FIVE: *The Medical Mission*
Mission Doctors Association Website. http://missiondoctors.org/history/.

CHAPTER SIX: *Love for the Win*
Beck, Glenn. "Lauren Hill Shares Her Incredible Story with Glenn." The Blaze TV (video), November 6, 2014.

Benjamin, Dan. "Coach Dan Benjamin Reflects on Year with Lauren Hill." WCPO Cincinnati, April 7, 2015.

Cohen, Paula. "Lauren Hill, Inspirational College Basketball Player with Cancer, Dead at 19." CBS News, April 10, 2015.

Daugherty, Paul. "Facing Death, Lauren Hill Teaches Us Life Lessons," *USA Today*, October 27, 2014.

———. "Lauren Hill: 'I want everybody to know I never give up.'" *Cincinnati Enquirer*, April 10, 2015.

Delle Donne, Elena. "Elena Delle Donne Reflects on Lauren Hill." WNBA, http://www.wnba.com/archive/wnba/sky/news/lauren_hill_game_recap_2014.html.

Loreno, Darcie. "Inspirational Ohio Basketball Player, Lauren Hill, Passes Away After Battle with Cancer." Fox8 Cleveland, April 10, 2015.

Martin, Sami K. "Brittany Maynard Ends Her Life: 'Spread Good Energy. Pay It Forward' She Writes in Final Post," *Christian Post*, November 3, 2014.

Payne, Marissa. "LeBron James to Lauren Hill: 'You inspired me,'" *Washington Post*, April 10, 2015.

Rinaldi, Tom. "Lauren Hill: One More Game." ESPN (video), August 6, 2015.

CHAPTER SEVEN: *A Home of Hope*
Dunigan, Christina. "A Dose of Reality," Real Choice. August 14, 2007. http://realchoice.blogspot.com/2007/08/dose-of-reality.html.

Mother's Home. "About Us." http://mothershome.org/about-us/.

Slobodzian, Joseph A. "Saving a Life vs. Honoring a Will a Doctor's Family Sued for 'Wrongful Life.' a Judge Sided with the Hospital," *Philadelphia Inquirer*, August 20, 1999.

Smith, Nadia Maria. "Doctor Creates Calendar to Benefit Mothers' Home." CatholicPhilly.com. http://catholicphilly. com/2008/12/news/local-news/local-catholic-news/ doctor-creates-calendar-to-benefit-mothers-home/.

CHAPTER EIGHT: *Save My School*
This story originally appeared in the *National Catholic Register* on June 16, 2012, as "How a Little Boy Saved a Catholic School."
Geromichalos, Tommy. "Tommy's Wish." St. Cyril of Alexandria. http://www.saintcyril.org/tommyswish.htm.

CHAPTER NINE: *The Unexpected Miracle*
Subject exclusive interviews with the author provided the basis for this story.

CHAPTER TEN: *A Man and His Rosary*
This story originally appeared in the *National Catholic Register* on October 27, 2011, as "Town Rejects Rosary as Offensive and the Prayers That Changed Everything."
Heslam, Jessica. "Upton Selectmen Denied Request for Rosary Rally," *Boston Herald*, October 27, 2011.
———. "Upton Sees the Light on Rosary Vigil," *Boston Herald*, October 28, 2011.
The Town Crier. http://www.towncrier.us/about-us.php.

CHAPTER ELEVEN: *Fighting the Deadly Silence*
"Born Alive Infants Protection Act—President Bush Signs / Pro-Life Anti-Abortion Video." YouTube video, 5:36, posted by rosaryfilms, August 9, 2008. https://www.youtube.com/ watch?v=6Mmi-Ul4iqo.
Christian Life Resources. "Nationally Renowned Pro-Life Nurse Fired from Christ Hospital Job." September 3, 2001.
McCann, Tom. "Hospital Fires Critic of Abortion Procedure," *Chicago Tribune*, September 3, 2001.
Roeser, Thomas. "Score 2 for Pro-Life Forces," *Chicago Sun-Times*, July 27, 2002.

Stanek, Jill. "Dr. Koop Opposed Eugenic Abortions at Christ Hospital." JillStanek.com. February 27, 2013. http://www.jillstanek.com/2013/02/dr-koop-opposed-eugenic-abortions-at-christ-hospital/.

———. "Testimony of Jill Stanek RN IL Health and Human Services." Jill Stanek.com. March 12, 2003.

Zanoza, Dan. "Subject Exclusive from RFM News Jill Stanek testimony on live-birth abortion." Choose Life. March 27, 2001. http://www.pathlights.com/abortion/abortion_news_p7.htm.

CHAPTER TWELVE: *Victim 0001*

Burger, John. "Father Judge, a Hero, Died a Hero's Death," *National Catholic Register*, September 23, 2001.

Duffy, Fr. Michael. "'The Happiest Man on Earth,' The Eulogy for Father Mychal Judge," Beliefnet.com, September, 2006. http://www.beliefnet.com/Wellness/2006/09/The-Happiest-Man-On-Earth-The-Eulogy-For-Father-Mychal-Judge. aspx?p=1#are6s0jX2XM34k7r.99.

Ford, Michael. *Father Mychal Judge: An Authentic American Hero*. Boston: Paulist, 2002.

Goodman, Amy. "Saint of 9/11: Remembering NY Fire Chaplain Mychal Judge, Gay Catholic Priest Killed at WTC," Democracy Now. September 6, 2011. http://www.democracynow. org/2011/9/6/saint_of_9_11_remembering_ny.

Judge, Fr. Mychal. "The Last Homily of Fr. Mychal Judge." Quoted in *Mychal's Message*, September 10, 2001. http://www.mychalsmessage.org/aboutfrm/homily.htm.

Walters, Kerry. *Profiles in Christian Courage: Extraordinary Inspiration for Everyday Life*. Lanham, MD: Rowman & Littlefield, 2014.

CHAPTER THIRTEEN: *Losing Fear*

Mercer, Heather, and Dayna Curry. *Prisoners of Hope: The Story of Our Captivity and Freedom in Afghanistan*. Colorado Springs: Waterbrook, 2003.

Morgan, Timothy. "How Heather Mercer's Hostage Stint Turned into Global Hope: After 9/11, the Missionary's Ten-Year Journey Leads from the Taliban to Iraqi Kurdistan," *Christianity Today*, September 12, 2011.

CHAPTER FOURTEEN: *The Friend of My Final Moment*

Blosser, Christopher. "The Monk-Martyrs of Tibhirine," The American Catholic. February 27, 2011. http://the-american-catholic.com/2011/02/27/the-monk-martyrs-of-tibhirine/.

"Gospel Reading of the Day," Carry the Gospel with You. Cacina. March 27, 2013. https://cacina.wordpress.com/2013/03/27/carry-the-gospel-with-you-1561/.

Hampson, Rick. "The Martyr's Testament: Seven monks write testimony to how their Christian faith was severely tested," *Associated Press/Luddington Daily News*. March 29, 1997, pg. 4.

Kiser, John. *The Monks of Tibhirine: Faith, Love, and Terror in Algeria*. New York: Macmillan, 2003.

Kun, Jeanne. "The Trappist Martyrs of Algiers," *Sword of the Spirit*. October, 2011. http://www.swordofthespirit.net/bulwark/october2011p4.htm.

Martin, Fr. James. "Dom Christian's Testament," *America*, November 14, 2015.

Pennington, M. Basil, OSCO. "Cistercian Martyrs of Algeria, 1996," *Review for Religious*, November-December, 1996.

Royal, Robert. "Faith, Terror and Martyrdom in Algeria: The Monks of Tibhirine," GodSpy. http://oldarchive.godspy.com/issues/Faith-Terror-and-Martyrdom-in-Algeria-The-Monks-of-Tibhirine.cfm.html.

———. "Seeing Things: Seven Modern Martyrs," *Crisis*, June 1, 2002.

CHAPTER FIFTEEN: *Kneeling on the Fifty-Yard Line*

Broom, Jack. "Bremerton Coach's Prayers Catch Attention of Congress," *Seattle Times*, October 27, 2015.

Calkins, Matt. "Why Bremerton Coach Joe Kennedy's Stance on Postgame Prayer Is Admirable," *Seattle Times*, October 15, 2015.

Clarridge, Christine. "Crowd Prays with Coach as he Defies School District," *Seattle Times*, October 16, 2015.

Hanna, Jason, and Steve Almasy. "Washington High School Coach Placed on Leave for Praying on Field," *CNN*. October 30, 2015. http://www.cnn.com/2015/10/29/us/washington-football-coach-joe-kennedy-prays/.

Liberty Institute. "Liberty Institute Files Federal EEOC Complaint Against Bremerton School District on Behalf of Coach Joe Kennedy." December 17, 2015. http://blog.libertyinstitute.org/2015/12/liberty-institute-files-federal.html.

"Praying Coach Watches Final Home Game from Sidelines as Suspension Continues," UpNorthLive.com. October 30, 2015. http://upnorthlive.com/news/nation-world/praying-coach-watches-final-home-game-from-sidelines-suspension-continues.

"State Schools Chief Says Coach's Midfield Prayer Can Be 'Exclusionary or Even Distressing' to Players," Q13Fox, October 23, 2015. http://q13fox.com/2015/10/23/state-superintendent-weighs-in-on-bremerton-coachs-post-game-prayer/.

Rosoff, Henry. "Coach Resumes Prayer on Field, Awaits District Reaction," KIRO7.com. October 16, 2015. http://www.kirotv.com/news/news/bremerton-school-district-responds-defense-praying/nn4wM/.

"Satanists Offer Prayer Services to Students, Staff at Bremerton High School," MYNorthwest.com. October 26, 2015. http://mynorthwest.com/?sid=2834446&nid=651.

"Sen. Lankford, Rep. Forbes: Let Coach Kennedy Remain Free to Pray, as We Are in Congress," Fox News Opinion. October 28, 2015. http://www.foxnews.com/opinion/2015/10/28/sen-lankford-rep-forbes-let-coach-kennedy-remain-free-to-pray-as-are-in-congress.html.

Starnes, Todd. "Time for a Hail Mary? School Threatens to Fire Praying Football Coach," CharismaNews. October 26, 2015. http://www.charismanews.com/opinion/american-dispatch/52838-time-for-a-hail-mary-school-threatens-to-fire-praying-football-coach.

Tan, Avianne. "HS Football Coach Vows to Continue Prayers Over Objections," ABC News. October 15, 2015. http://abcnews.go.com/US/hs-football-coach-vows-continue-prayers-objections/story?id=34495965.

CHAPTER SIXTEEN: *Miracle Gianna*

Baldwin, Lou. "A Family Brought Together by God," CatholicPhilly.com. December 10, 2009. http://catholicphilly.com/2009/12/news/local-news/local-catholic-news/a-family-brought-together-by-god/.

———. "Confrontation turns to breakthrough," CatholicPhilly.com. March 18, 2010. http://catholicphilly.com/2010/03/news/local-news/local-catholic-news/confrontation-turns-to-breakthrough/.

Bucks County Pro-Life Coalition. "Miracle Gianna Has Gone to Heaven," February 5, 2010. http://www.buckscountyprolife.com/articles/miracle-gianna-has-gone-to-heaven.html.

"Mission and Values." St. Mary Medical Center. http://www.stmaryhealthcare.org/body.cfm?id=6.

"Our Staff: Lester A. Ruppersberger, D.O.," Center for Women's Health. http://www.ctrforwomenshealth.com/our-staff.html#ruppersberger.

Zuhlsdorf, Fr. John. "Prepare to be amazed! The 2nd miracle of St. Gianna Molla," Fr. Z's Blog. April 28, 2012. http://wdtprs.com/blog/2012/04/prepare-to-be-amazed-the-2nd-miracle-of-st-gianna-molla-2/.

CHAPTER SEVENTEEN: *The Wedding Cake*

"A Christian woman's testimony of her husband's martyrdom," Vatican Radio. December 17, 2015. http://en.radiovaticana.

va/news/2015/12/17/a__christian_womans_testimony_of_her_
husbands_martyrdom/1195085.

Anderson, Ryan T. *Truth Overruled: The Future of Marriage and
Religious Freedom*. Washington, D.C.: Regnery, 2015.

"Cake artist asks Colo. Supreme Court to affirm his freedom of
expression," Alliance Defending Freedom. October 23, 2015.
http://www.adfmedia.org/News/PRDetail/8700.

McIntyre, Ken. "24 Questions for Jack Phillips, the Baker Who
Gave Up Wedding Cakes for God," *The Daily Signal*. August
19, 2015. http://dailysignal.com/2015/08/19/24-questions-for-
jack-phillips-the-baker-who-gave-up-wedding-cakes-for-god/.

Mena, Adelaide. "Christian Baker Files Religious-Freedom
Appeal in Wedding-Cake Ruling," *National Catholic Register*,
January 9, 2014.

Osborn, Katy. "Colorado Baker Appeals Ruling Over Same-Sex
Wedding Cake," *Time*, July 7, 2015.

Starnes, Todd. "Colorado Double Standard: Bakers Should
Not Be Forced to Make Anti-Gay Cakes," Todd's American
Dispatch. *FoxNews*. April 07, 2015. http://www.foxnews.com/
opinion/2015/04/07/colorado-double-standard-bakers-should-
not-be-forced-to-make-anti-gay-cakes.html.

CHAPTER EIGHTEEN: *Losing All but Not Everything*

Allen, John, Jr. "The New Christian Martyrs: In India and across
Asia, Christians Are Targeted for Their Faith," Crux. December
20, 2015. http://www.cruxnow.com/faith/2015/12/20/.
in-india-and-across-asia-christians-are-targeted-for-their-faith/.

Nayak, Mrs. Kanak Rekha. "How the Eucharist Changed My
Life." National Eucharistic Congress. http://www.nation-
aleucharisticcongress.in/testimonials/kanak-rekha-nayak.

ABOUT THE AUTHOR

Matthew Archbold is a professional journalist, blogger, and columnist for *Catholic Digest* and *National Catholic Register.* He and his brother Patrick produce the Creative Minority Report.